ENDORSEMENTS

The genius of Christianity, commented one theologian, lies in making primary matters secondary and secondary matters primary. In this scholarly and passionately written book, Don Milam redirects our attention to all that really matters.

Brennan Manning
Author, *A Glimpse of Jesus: A Stranger to Self-Hatred*

In this extraordinary book, Don Milam has done it again; he has made the language of God both amazingly simple and astoundingly profound. Love and grace are the language of God and "the ancient language of Eden." Every believer should read and comprehend the heart of the message contained in this book. What we preach may be forgotten, but what is written shall live on for future generations. *The Ancient Language of Eden* is a treasure for the present and the future. I highly recommend the book and the author.

Bishop David R. Huskins, Th.D., D.D.
Fellowship of Vineyard Harvester Churches

With the writing of *The Ancient Language of Eden*, Don Milam has done a great service for the Body of Christ. It is a magnificent book destined to blow away the smog of religiosity clouding the simplicity of the gospel. *The Ancient Language of Eden* is written clearly for this generation that seems to have lost its way. It provides a roadmap back to the place and the presence we all long to experience.

Dr. Mark Hanby
Mark Hanby Ministries

This is a handbook about spiritual rebirth and revival. Not the theory, but the way into it. From the first page, *The Ancient Language of Eden* drips with the Presence that salts the soul's thirst for Him and breathlessly waits for the encounter! As you read, the encounter begins. It is filled with bursts of revelation that will astound and overwhelm you, seeding your soul with glimpses of glory that linger for months. Inspired and intelligent, *The Ancient Language of Eden* is a compass for seekers of every age and tongue. Beautifully done from a heart of experience with a Living God that transcends religion and touches His glory, *The Ancient Language of Eden* evokes a deep-unto-deep opening to God. Don Milam lets us realize we are the ink that wets the pen of the Greatest Story Teller, and He is inscribing each of us on the pages of His autobiography. In the same spirit of the mystics, the influence of *The Ancient Language of Eden* is a timely masterpiece set to become a benchmark classic in Christian reflection and disciplines of the spirit that will extend well beyond our day.

Mahesh and Bonnie Chavda
All Nations Church

I was held captive by Don Milam's rediscovery of "the ancient language of Eden." As I read this book, which I think will become a classic in the libraries of those who are hungry for God. Don is a man that has learned "the ancient language of Eden" so well he can communicate to us who are trapped behind the high walls of manipulative theologies and human effort. His journey is like that of an Indiana Jones who has discovered, and wants to share with the world, his priceless find. It is priceless because like Paul, he had to count all of what he was as nothing, in order to truly possess this rare artifact of grace.

Pastor Cleddie Keith
Heritage Christian Fellowship

This book weaves together a tapestry of "scandalous love!" Grace will once again become no less than amazing as you rediscover "the ancient language of Eden." Get ready to encounter the God of Love and meet Him between the lines. Get ready to be ruined by His heart!

Jill Austin
Founder of Master Potter Ministries
Author, *Master Potter* and *Master Potter and the Mountain of Fire*

Easily understood, yet profoundly deep, *The Ancient Language of Eden* is one of the clearest portrayals of God's love relationship with man—the crown of His creation—that I have ever read. If you are in search of food that will satisfy your soul, like that of an evening enjoying a delightful seven course meal with your most intimate friend, then you will devour this feast. Written from a pen of a transparent life, Don Milam breaks the bread of the master and of his own life in a manner that will compel you to come running into the arms of our Father's embrace.

Jim W. Goll
Cofounder of Ministry to the Nations
Author, *The Lost Art of Intercession* and *Wasted on Jesus*

THE ANCIENT
LANGUAGE OF EDEN

Rediscovering the Original Language
of Jesus—Love, Grace, and Mercy

DON MILAM

Destiny Image® Publishers, Inc.
P.O. Box 310
Shippensburg, PA 17257-0310

"Discovering the Fullness of the Deeper Life."

ISBN 0-7684-2162-4

For Worldwide Distribution
Printed in the U.S.A.

This book and all other Destiny Image, Revival Press, MercyPlace,
Fresh Bread, Destiny Image Fiction, and Treasure House books
are available at Christian bookstores and distributors worldwide.

3 4 5 6 7 8 9 10 / 06 05

To place a book order, call toll-free: **1-800-722-6774**.
For more information on foreign distributors, call **717-532-3040**.
Or reach us on the Internet:
www.destinyimage.com

CONTENTS

FOREWORD

The prevailing conditions of our world today are the source of much fear, anxiety, disillusionment, frustration, insecurity, and depression. The political leaders, social architects, economic gurus, scientific wizards, educational professionals, and philosophical geniuses seem to be bankrupt of ideas to respond to the global challenges. The 21st century seems to have led our planet on a course toward self-destruction like a galactic space ship without a compass.

It seems like all our technological, scientific, and social advancements have not been able to solve our human problems. The reality is that today there are more wars and conflicts than in any other time in history. We have invented everything, except a way to solve the disease in the human heart. The result continues to be political corruption, economic insecurity, racial strife, ethnic cleansing, escalating violent crimes, drug wars, the proliferation of gangs, and religious wars. What is the answer to the global dilemma?

The answer to our future is in an ancient language, a language that invaded earth at the beginning of creation. We need a revival of the language of love, grace and mercy.

Don Milam's *The Ancient Language of Eden*, in his very simple yet profound way presents a fresh look at a subject that the 21st century world is dying to receive. In this work, Don leaps over complicated theological jargon and presents the fundamental precepts of the missing ingredients for our world today. The overworked concept of love is once again placed back into its divine context so that we can speak the language of God again.

His treatment of the "grace factor," is superb and will drive you back to the heart of God for more. His exploration of the concept

9

of "mercy" is a missing component that even the church needs to rediscover.

This book is destined to be a classic and should be read and in the library of every individual who desires to find answers to the many challenges of our post-modern world. I highly congratulate Don on another masterpiece and see it as a timeless contribution to this and future generations.

Dr. Myles Munroe
BFM International
Nassau, Bahamas

ACKNOWLEDGMENTS

In his famous lecture on spiritual change, Henry Drummond said that the pyramid of humanity is built upon the power of influence. He is right; no man is an island. We are all the result of the many influences that have come into our lives. Very little in our world results from pure originality. The books we have read, the things we have heard, and the people we have known have all left an indelible impression upon us. *The Ancient Language of Eden* is the result of the many influences that have come into my life over the years. It would be impossible to list all of those influences. Suffice it to say that they are many.

After a year or so of contemplating and studying the Scriptures on the truths of the ancient language of Eden, I was introduced to the writings of S.D. Gordon. I was amazed when I read these words on the first page: "Jesus is God spelling Himself out so man can understand. He is the A and the Z, and all between, of the Old Eden language of love." I had imagined that my thoughts on the ancient language were unique, but at that moment I was reminded again that there is nothing new under the sun.

The writings of Henry Drummond, S.D. Gordon, Rufus M. Jones, Dorothy Sayers, Robert Farrar Capon, Brennan Manning, Hans Kung, and many others have left their imprint on the linings of my soul. I give honor to them and the spiritual discoveries they have made. They have assisted Micki and I greatly in our own spiritual pursuit. Their words have inspired us and given us courage for the journey.

I would also like to recognize my wife, Micki. She has been my traveling companion, and together we have rejoiced in the discoveries we have made over the last few years. We have been overwhelmed by the outrageous nature of Father's love. Micki has also labored hard with this manuscript, giving it a more personal and living touch. I am the teacher and she is the romantic.

And if there is a God who can take the dead and, without a single condition of credit-worthiness or a single, point-less promise of reform, raise them up whole and forgiven, free for nothing—well, that would not only be wild and wonderful; it would be the single piece of Good News in a world drowning in an ocean of blame.[1]
He forgets our sins in the darkness of the tomb. He finds us, in short, in the desert of death, not in the garden of improvement; and in the power of Jesus' resurrection, he puts us on his shoulders rejoicing and brings us home.[2]

Robert Farrar Capon

The recovery of passion begins with the recovery of my true self as the beloved. If I find Christ I will find myself and if I find my true self I will find Him. This is the goal and purpose of our lives.[3]

Brennan Manning

CHAPTER 1

DISCOVERING THE
ANCIENT LANGUAGE

More than 40 years ago I was born, or I should say born again. In the joy of this new experience I looked for opportunities to tell my friends what had happened to me. I didn't have the right words to explain this profound experience, and I am sure they did not understand a thing I said. I was just a babe and couldn't describe my faith very well. It became clear to me that I needed to be trained.

I went to Bible college and diligently worked to fully understand the faith in order to communicate more clearly the truths of the Bible. I was so excited to arrive at this respected school of learning. They would surely train me in the *linguistics* of Christianity. For the next four years professors skilled in the nuances of this incredible language instructed me in all the details of the faith. Under their tutelage I replaced the "baby talk" of my born-again experience with a more sophisticated style of speaking, guaranteeing I would impress and win the unlearned.

My speech improved day by day, it seemed, and I was quickly adding new and weighty words to my vocabulary. I learned the deep meanings and hidden fine distinctions of such weighty words as justification, redemption, sanctification, predestination, and glorification. I thrived on the difficult subjects of ecclesiology, hermeneutics, eschatology, and soteriology. While it was not easy, I pressed on to become fairly proficient in this complex language. I was energized. This was, indeed, the right course for my life.

I especially loved my courses in homiletics. (If you are unfamiliar with theological language, homiletics teaches you how to make complicated Bible truths simple enough for the untrained.) I was taught how to skillfully study the Scriptures, create outlines, and add enlightening descriptions developed from proper exegesis of the Scriptures. (Exegesis simply means finding the hidden meaning of the Greek text). The necessity of introducing illustrations to stir the emotions was encouraged. And I learned one should always conclude a sermon with a resounding challenge to the people, while their emotions were still running high.

The importance of public speaking principles was emphasized. Body movements, the cadence of the voice, proper articulation of words, and eye contact would help to achieve the desired response. I could almost daily feel the power of the new language growing within me.

As I heard missionaries share the great needs around the world, I became convinced God wanted me to serve Him in a foreign land. After all, He needed me and others like me to teach the nations the ways of Christianity. Those four years of Bible training were strenuous and demanding, but I thrived on all the intellectual learning. My heart wanted so much to serve the Lord and teach others the wonderful things I was learning. I felt ready to test my wings in the real world by telling people the Good News.

A Call to Foreign Lands

Following graduation in 1968 and my marriage to Micki, whom I had met in Bible college, I went to work with Teen Challenge in the inner city of Philadelphia. I felt ready for this hour. All my classes and thousands of hours of studies had prepared me with the answers to the questions of the lost. Passing out tracts and witnessing on the streets netted us some results, but to my consternation, nothing like I had hoped for.

There was one outreach setting that I found to be particularly challenging and somewhat overwhelming at times. Teen Challenge ran a coffee shop in a small, dingy basement near Rittenhouse Square in downtown Philadelphia. In the mid- to late-'60s this park and surrounding area was home to a mixture of hippies, drug addicts, prostitutes and their pimps, gang members, alcoholics—all rubbing shoulders with intellectuals from the University of Pennsylvania, Villanova University, and Temple University.

In those early days, I felt ready for the challenge of these pseudo intellectuals. After all, I knew the truth. Eagerly, I threw myself into the coffee house ministry. As I sat down those evenings at a small table, sipping coffee with my Bible in front of me, I confronted the best and the worst the world had to offer. As they poured out their philosophies of humanism, expressing open disdain and often-outright hatred of God, I tried to persuade them that the god of this world had blinded them. All they needed to do was admit they were wrong and make the leap of faith. God would catch them.

It didn't take long for me to realize that I was totally out of my depth. Lost in a maze of existentialism and philosophical profundities, my head was spinning with the words of Sartre, Nietzsche, and Freud thrown at me night after night. Why weren't they asking the questions to which I had the carefully prepared answers? I felt like I had wandered into a foreign land where I was surrounded by voices speaking a language that I didn't know.

Perplexed and shaken to the core at the end of those interminable hours, I returned each evening to the security of our center, where I felt relief in familiar surroundings. I felt like I had stumbled into an alien landscape peopled by strange and often hostile beings. The Teen Challenge Center became my sanctuary in this alien environment.

It was only much later in my life that I became aware that, in fact, something was happening in the heavens at that time. During that period of my life when I was safely ensconced in Bible college, powerful changes were taking place in our culture. Having survived two world wars, mankind had passed into an era characterized by cynicism and disillusionment, expressed in a growing rebellion against all forms of authority. I was living in seclusion somewhat oblivious to those changes.

In those early days of ministry in Philadelphia, I was becoming increasingly disgusted with this exaltation of man and convinced myself that the little fruit being produced from my ministry was not due to any deficiency in myself. Their intellectualism prevented these lost ones from understanding the truth of the Gospel. They just didn't have the faith to accept my theological reasoning. But deep in my heart, I was having a hard time accepting the logic of my position.

My ineffectiveness in convincing them of "the way" troubled me greatly. Unknown to me, a seed of doubt had taken root in my spirit. This seed would continue to grow in the years to come. Why did the language of the Church not attract and convince those beyond the walls of the Church? Had the world changed so much over the centuries, or had the Church and its ways become irrelevant and impotent to affect change in the hearts of men? I was only a couple of years into the ministry and already was questioning things I had learned about it.

Off to the Mission Field

After our less than satisfying time in Teen Challenge we left the States to study Portuguese in Lisbon, preparing to follow our dream of serving God in Africa. With renewed enthusiasm we launched out for the foreign fields. Micki, our two small children, and I sailed for the country of Mozambique.

Upon our arrival it was love at first sight. In spite of being under white domination for hundreds of years, the people of Mozambique were a gracious and accepting people. We anticipated the joy of spending the rest of our lives preaching the Gospel in this beautiful land.

The three years we spent in Mozambique were filled with a kaleidoscope of shifting emotions. Our first shock was when we found that our mission field leader had a totally different vision and agenda for us—much different than we were sensing by the Spirit. Having been trained to submit to leadership, we tried cooperating and submitting to his direction, trusting that God would fulfill His plans for us. But as the months went by, to our consternation our path continued to diverge further and further from that of our leader. Finally the Lord released us to sever our ties with the mission, promising us His provision.

Around the time that our third child was born, the Lord sovereignly opened a door that had us in total awe. In a Catholic country with bare tolerance for Protestant mission work, I was asked by the Minister of Health of Mozambique to open and operate a drug rehabilitation program to combat the massive drug problems of the country. Never in my wildest dreams could I have anticipated such a thing, but it was God's dream, and I was living in it.

Without giving the details, I'll just say that God worked miracles and we soon found ourselves with a center, several staff members, and a number of the main drug runners of the country living under its roof. It was a time of great excitement and fulfillment. Even then, however, the joy I experienced was tainted by a growing disillusionment over what I observed firsthand of the ministry.

Micki and I had a missionary friend who regularly went into the city hospital to minister to Portuguese soldiers, many who had been wounded severely in the war of liberation going on in the North. The story she related to us fed the flame of doubt silently smoldering within me. On one of her visits to the hospital she approached the bedside of a badly wounded young soldier and asked him how he was doing. A simple question, but his answer pierced her soul.

"Do you really care how I am? Or are you like the rest of those Christians who come in here looking for another notch on their gun? They ask us how we are and before we can even respond, they begin telling us we're sinners and need to repent or we're going to hell."

What an indictment! Was that how the world viewed our good deeds? Was that how they saw me? Even more disturbingly was the thought that *my* motivation in the work of the ministry was to put notches on *my* gun. Did I really love the lost, or was I just being busy for God, so I could feel good about myself?

The Beginning of Dark Days— Ten Months in a Communist Prison

When Micki and I were preparing to come to Mozambique as missionaries, we knew that the Portuguese colonialists had been in an ongoing struggle with freedom fighters in the North of this beautiful country. Frelimo, the communist-backed rebel group, had been waging a guerilla-type war for independence. This had been going on for so long, people took it in stride. In the South, where we lived in the capital city, life went on in a relatively normal fashion. We saw little fear in the people we worked among or in other missionaries.

In 1974 the unimaginable happened. The military in Portugal successfully effected a *coup d'etat* against the government, and the first thing the new junta did was give independence to their three African colonies. A year later, in June of 1975, Frelimo celebrated Mozambique's independence with jeeps of soldiers firing their automatic weapons into the air in the streets of Lourenco Marques.

At the urging of the U.S. Consulate, most American missionaries left, but Micki and I and our staff sought the Lord for direction and felt it was right for us to stay. The people we had been ministering to and come to love had no place to go for sanctuary. We could not leave them.

One month after Independence Day I was arrested and taken to the police station. I was questioned for six hours and had no way of knowing that two of our staff workers were being interrogated in another room. Later that evening I was put in a military jeep and driven to my home. Several soldiers woke my wife and children as they searched our house, waving their weapons. I didn't know what they were looking for and had only a minute to quickly whisper to Micki that it would be all right. This was just a big misunderstanding, and once they realized it, I would be back home.

By then it was about ten o'clock at night, and I was brusquely ordered back outside and into the jeep. I was taken to the ominous-looking military prison. Arriving in the dark of night, I was processed and led to cell number six in prison block A. Dazed, I found myself secured with two other prisoners.

"Oh God, where are You?" I cried out. No answer seemed to come.

That was the first of the 300 nights I would spend in that dark, fear-filled, concrete prison. I had prepared my whole adult life to serve the Lord in this very country where I now found myself imprisoned. My lifelong dream had turned into a nightmare. I was confused and depressed. Where was God, and how could He let this happen? My earlier confidence that this was all a mistake began to evaporate. What was going to happen to Micki and my three small children with chaos and violence escalating in the destabilized country? Horror stories of the unrestrained actions of the guerillas turned "policemen" filtered into the prison daily.

Gradually I numbly settled into the daily routine of prison life. From the very first day, the prison guards expressed great antipathy for all the foreigners under their care. The first morning I was dragged by the soldiers into the mess hall and ordered to take off my shoes, get on my knees, and wash the floor with a brush. This was the first of many humiliations. I came to dread the times when the whole prison population was brought together and made to watch while certain inmates were beaten and tortured. As a sheltered American, I was shocked at the total disregard for human life these cruel jailers had.

Adding to my ragged emotional state of mind was the fear for my family living on the outside. They were trying to get by in those tumultuous days. Single women were being targeted by roving bands of ex-guerillas, now soldiers. Food was scarce. Homes were being broken into and robbed of all belongings. On one stormy night while my wife and children were sleeping, our home was broken into and all our belongings were stripped from us. My mind was racked with a deep sense of helplessness to protect them.

In the midst of the dark cloud of fear and uncertainty that hung over me, I became aware of a quiet but powerful energy at work *in* me. I think this was the first time I experientially came to know the force we call *grace*. While I was not always conscious of this power, it was there and it was working. Grace was empowering me for this moment. At times I could literally feel the warmth of God's presence sweeping over the cold gripping my soul. More often, though, I felt like such a failure and would be almost overwhelmed by depression. I was plagued by the question, "What had I done wrong to deserve this imprisonment?"

Grace in a Prison Cell

The Frelimo soldiers who were the official guards over the prison looked for ways to frighten and humiliate the foreigners. Toward the end of my time in prison, their fear tactics increased. One Sunday they burst into my cell and hauled me and six or seven other prisoners into the prison courtyard. Handing each one of us a shovel and herding us to the middle of the courtyard, they sharply commanded us to start digging.

After digging for nearly four hours we stood in a massive hole whose lip was over our heads. During this whole time the soldiers, who were high on marijuana, yelled and waved their AK-47s threateningly over our heads. Finally they screamed at us to climb out of the hole, whereupon they lined us up with the gaping hole at our heels and their fierce countenances in front. I wondered if this might be the end. I was never going home; I was never going to see my family again.

With our eyes tightly closed, we heard the frightening sound of weapons being loaded. I stood resigned, waiting for the bullets that were going to end the horror. Nothing! Suddenly a wild fit of laughter broke the silence. Immediately they started shoving us toward the prison doors. It took me some time to realize that I was still alive. I had survived another life-threatening encounter in this nightmare.

Where was grace during these moments? As I said, the power of grace was not always obvious, but deep within I still knew that a spiritual energy was keeping me through each moment of this greatest challenge of my life. It was very clear that it was not the things I had learned through studies of the Scriptures, as great as they were, that were keeping me and saving me. It was the power of God's wonderful grace—a very real power outside myself that was strengthening me in these awful days. I had certainly done nothing to deserve it. Grace was there, wrapping me in its warm embrace.

The storm finally passed. After ten months of never knowing if I was going to live or die, in May of 1976 I was expelled from Mozambique under miraculous circumstances—never to return. Joyously reunited with my family in Pennsylvania, I shook off the fear that had been my companion for 300 days and was ready to begin a new life. I began working in the church my father was pastoring, and for the next ten years I was involved in local church ministry. This was a brand new experience. All I had known in the past was evangelism, but I quickly set myself to learn all I needed to become a successful pastor.

I started reading everything I could get my hands on. I read Watchman Nee, Dietrich Bonhoeffer, E. Stanley Jones, Philip Yancey, DeVerne Fromke, Howard Snyder, T. Austin Sparks, and many others. New words were being added almost daily to my vocabulary: Kingdom of God, fivefold ministry, body ministry, spiritual gifts, servanthood, house church, apostolic and prophetic ministry. The things I was learning gave me a new sense of purpose and spiritual power, making me feel important in the things of God.

I loved the feelings I experienced when I preached the Word, sharing with others the wonderful spiritual truths that were unfolding to me. A new sense of identity as a child of God was being formed in me. Someone once had told me that the person who has the most knowledge has the most power. I deeply believed this: increasing my knowledge would empower me for God's work. Knowledge became the focus of my life.

The Dark Night of the Soul

I did not understand it at the time, but by throwing myself into spiritual activity, I was unconsciously seeking to eradicate the nagging sense of insecurity and disenchantment that was once more plaguing me. For a season, the combination of book knowledge and spiritual activity created a delusion of spiritual security and acceptance by God. From time to time I would feel a strong inexplicable urge rise up within me to get out of the ministry, but I was afraid to give in to it. It was a crazy thought! After all, I knew nothing but ministry. How would I support my family if I set it aside? What would I do?

Caught in a downward spiral, I spent unimaginable amounts of energy simply trying to suppress these thoughts. I felt like I was locked up in another kind of prison, almost more frightening than the one in which I had spent ten horrifying months.

This inner disillusionment eventually climaxed when a series of ministry crises crashed down on Micki and me. One heartbreaking day I awoke to find that while I was taken up with trying to find my place in the ministry, my family had shipwrecked on the rocks of life and was in pieces. Our children had been young when we uprooted them not just once but numerous times. Still, Micki and I thought they were okay because we loved them deeply and committed them to God's keeping. However, when they were in their teen years, the moves and instability of life took their toll. Each of our beloved children eventually spent their own time in prison as a result of some disastrous choices.

We were devastated at what we perceived to be our inexcusable failure to care for our own lambs because we were so busy caring for God's sheep. In inexpressible pain and desperation, with no real plan for the future, my wife and I resigned from the church we were pastoring. In total disillusionment with the ministry, I turned my back on it and found a job as a painter (a good occupation for wayward preachers). To my surprise, I found I was very good at it. It was mindless labor and that's all I wanted at that point. I wish I could say that getting out of the ministry saved my family, but it didn't. We spent the next seven or eight years in the darkest time of our lives (including our experience in Mozambique).

Our marriage was barely surviving the gut-wrenching blows that rained upon us on a regular basis. We walked through the valley with our children who had been left vulnerable by these events. In pain we cried out to the Lord. "God, we helped other parents rescue their kids from the dangers of this world. Why aren't You helping us? Why won't You answer our cries for help?" Where is the promise of your love and support? Why won't you talk to us?

We watched with broken hearts as our children were drawing further and further away from us and from God. I felt like I was sliding down a slippery slope, desperately grabbing for something, anything, to stop me. Micki and I prayed, cried, and raged at the unfairness of it all. Looking for some kind of answer, some key to open the heavens, we went through counseling, deliverance, and other forms of spiritual help. None of these spiritual tools worked.

The spiritual knowledge I had so diligently accumulated over the years provided no answers, nor could it alleviate the relentless pain we felt eating us up. My old religious language was slowly but steadily slipping away. I eventually lost all desire to use any of the once-loved words of that archaic religious vocabulary. It had failed us. It was only vain and hollow words that had no relevance to the realities of our devastated hearts and lives.

We eventually ran out of tears and released, one by one, all the religious exercises that we had once felt made us acceptable to our heavenly Father. We felt truly lost now!

Church could not help us and we certainly could not help ourselves. Littering the path behind us was Bible reading, church going, prayer, and fellowship with longtime Christian friends. Like so much extraneous gear weighing us down, we discarded all the spiritual activity once so necessary to us. By now the anger, depression, and confusion had buried us, leaving us spiritually numb and indifferent. We had already discarded all the answers we once had. With a deep sense of regret, we then gave up the questions. We had entered the "dark night of the soul" and had no idea if we would survive.

Jesus Loves Me, This I Know

For eight long years we endured the "silence" of heaven and the "empty words" of the Church. In silence we bore the shame of our failure. We drew into a cave, attempting to lick our wounds. Then one day, driving home from work, a deep sense of sorrow erupted out of my spirit, like a geyser bursting forth from the hard ground. Through a grief that threatened to undo me, I cried out to

God, "If only I knew You loved me! If I only knew! That love would change everything for me!"

The pain was overwhelming. I so longed to be free from the shame wrapped around me. I cried out to experience His love, but I felt my shame and guilt had created an insurmountable wall around me forever.

A few weeks later in the middle of a deep sleep, I heard these audible words, "Why are you robbing Me of My glory?" Even though it woke me up, I didn't know if I was dreaming or if I had actually heard something. The words came again, "Why are you robbing Me of My glory?" I waited. The third time I heard these words I was overwhelmed by a sense of awe and jumped out of bed. I knew God was there.

Strangely enough, His question did not come as a condemnation, but more like a deep desire for me. A glorious party was going on, but God was feeling a deep sense of loss because I was not there. He missed me? Could that be possible? I was the one who had failed in the heat of the battle. I had failed as a preacher, a husband, and a father. I surely must be a huge disappointment to God. Why in the world would He ever miss me?

I quietly got out of the bed so as not to disturb Micki and went down to the living room. Picking up my Bible for the first time in over a year, I began to read the following scriptures.

> *But we all, with unveiled face beholding as in a mirror the glory of the Lord, are being transformed into the same image from glory to glory, just as from the Lord, the Spirit.*
> 2 Corinthians 3:18

For God, who said, "Light shall shine out of darkness," is the One who has shone in our hearts to give the light of the knowledge of the glory of God in the face of Christ.

> *But we have this treasure in earthen vessels, that the surpassing greatness of the power may be of God and not from ourselves; persecuted, but not forsaken; struck down, but not destroyed.*   2 Corinthians 4:6,7

Powerful emotions began washing over me. The glory of His presence was shining like a great light around me. I could almost feel the arms of God drawing me to Himself, comforting my broken heart. I broke into uncontrollable weeping as His love washed over my soul again and again. For the first time in my life I truly understood He loved me. It was clear this love was not based on anything I had or had not done but was totally founded on who He was.

In that split second I experienced for the first time the inexplicable wonder of His marvelous grace. I stood there exposed before Him, as all my deep-rooted guilt and shame was washed away in a river of amazing grace. No words were needed! That morning I heard the first whisper of the ancient language of Eden. "Son, I love you. I always have!" I had passed through the dark night and was slowly emerging into the light of His amazing love.

> *O guiding light!*
> *O night more lovely than the dawn!*
> *O night that has united*
> *The Lover with His beloved*
> *Transforming the beloved in her Lover.*[4]

Introduction to the Ancient Language

My whole life had been built around attempting to please my dad and my God. Deep-seated humiliation had hounded me a good part of my life because I believed I was always doomed to fail. My Christian life had been based upon performance, and the day I took off my ministerial coat I was left "naked and ashamed." What hope did I have of pleasing God when I left the ministry, if I had never felt I had pleased Him when I was in the ministry?

I had been taught the Word of God, but I never had allowed the Word to teach me! I knew how to be a worker in the field, but I did not know how to be a lover in the house. I knew about the push of human effort, but I knew very little about the pull of divine grace. I had involved myself in a lot of spiritual activity, but I had soon learned it was all a religious cover-up. I had masked my insecurity and shame in a network of religious activity. I had thought I could gain His acceptance through the ministry. I did not realize that what I was always seeking, I already had. His love had always been there, free and unconditional.

Sitting there that morning, I cried like a child as I spoke my first words of the ancient language, "Jesus, I love you!" No impressive, flowery, religious verbiage. Just Don, crying out to Jesus, thanking Him for that long-desired love. He had climbed over the walls I had erected to protect myself from disappointment and pain. What I couldn't do, He did! The wonder of God's grace invaded my fortress of shame, and I succumbed to His outstretched arms. I was unashamedly *skinny dippin'* in a pool of amazing grace!

One other important issue was also resolved that day. During my entire Christian life, I had struggled with prayer and "quiet times." Whenever I would try to close myself off from the noise around me, the *voices* would begin. The voices of shame, guilt, and regret would start clamoring, disturbing any inward silence I had achieved. They would mercilessly remind me of my many failures as a minister, husband, and father. I felt powerless to combat these accusations because they were true. I *had* failed miserably. But the moment I jumped headfirst into that pool of grace, I discovered to my amazement that the voices were gone.

For the first time in my life the screams of shame were silenced. When I turned inward, all I heard was "sweet nothings" being whispered in the ears of my soul. I could not get enough of this divine attention. I was like an orphan who had just been adopted. I had craved this love and attention my whole life, but I always felt like a kid with his nose pressed up against the window of a candy store. It was only for others, not for the likes of me. Yet when I finally gave up even daring to hope that it could ever be mine, *it found me.*

In the days following that momentous morning, I couldn't get enough of the Gospels. I was like a starving man set down at a banquet. I read them over and over again. In my early years of Bible college and ministry, I had always been fascinated with the writings of Paul. After all, he was the one who held the *mystery* of building the Church. But this was not the time for more spiritual knowledge. My head was crammed full of spiritual truths and principles. I didn't need or want more information about the truth. I desperately thirsted for an experience *with* the Truth. Now was the time to discover Jesus!

The more I read the Gospels, the more amazed I became at the wonder and evidence of His love. I was undone by the constancy of His grace, the sweetness of His words, His magnetic attraction to those living on the outer fringes of society. I loved the way He shut the mouths of the cold and heartless religious leaders. It made me want to shout for joy!

I found myself wondering if I had ever known this Man. Where was the judge pointing his finger my way, his eyes filled with disappointment? I knew I had never known Him as I was seeing Him now, full of warmth and tenderness and compassion. I especially loved the Gospel of John. There was something about the intimacy of John's writings that overwhelmed me.

I was falling into the arms of Jesus, and I loved Him more than I knew how to express. Sometimes it seemed like a dream. Micki and I experienced moments of being afraid that we would wake up to find it was all some wonderful fantasy. But this was our reality...God had invaded our little space! I no longer cared about preaching or ministry. Perhaps this was selfishness, but I just wanted to know Him, to experience Him, to be with Him. My soul was being stretched beyond anything I could have imagined, and I never wanted it to return to its original size.

I felt like a baby, newly emerged from the womb, incapable of speech. All my past learning and religious jargon had been shed when I had passed through the birth canal of the dark night of the soul. The language of religion that I had spoken for so long had proved to be a false language, a dead language. It had failed me and had to be discarded.

I now discovered the original native tongue of every child of God. The language in the presence of Jesus was an ancient language, the one originally spoken in a primitive garden. I felt as though I was hearing the words whispered by God into the ear of Adam. Those delightful words, which began as a creative thought in the mind of a loving Creator, pulled me back to the beginning of all things.

Endnotes

1. *The Romance of the Word*, Robert Farrar Capon, Eerdmans, Grand Rapids, Michigan, 1995, p. 8.

2. *The Parables of Grace*, Robert Farrar Capon, Eerdmans, Grand Rapids, Michigan, 1988, p. 39.

3. *Abba's Child*, Brennan Manning, Navpress, Colorado Springs, Colorado, 1994, p. 123.

4. *The Dark Night of the Soul*, St. John of the Cross, www.ccel.org/j/john_of_the_cross/dark_night/dark_night_bod0.9.html#RTFToC44.

Between the idea
And the reality
Between the motion
And the act
Falls the Shadow
Between the conception
And the creation
Between the emotion
And the response
Falls the Shadow[1]

T.S. Eliot

Infinity of space is like a painter's table, prepared for the ground and field of those colours that are to be laid thereon. Look how great he intends the picture, so great doth he make the table. It would be an absurdity to leave it unfinished, or not to fill it. To leave any part of it naked and bare, and void of beauty, would render the whole ungrateful to the eye, and argue a defect of time or materials, or wit in the limner. As the table is infinite so are the pictures. God's Wisdom is the art, His Goodness the will, His Word the pencil, His Beauty and Power the colours, His Pictures are all His Works and Creatures. Infinitely more real and more glorious, as well as more great and manifold than the shadows of a landscape. But the Life of all is, they are the spectator's own. He is in them as in His territories, and in all these views His own possessions.[2]

Thomas Traherne

CHAPTER 2

IMAGE-MAKER AND THE
BEGINNING OF ALL THINGS

To understand the end of all things one must go back to the beginning of all things. There in the beginning are the answers to the questions troubling our empty souls, as well as a beautiful language we once spoke. All our searching for spiritual reality will eventually bring us to this quiet place inside the eastern gate. The final step in our search will take us right over the threshold of time into eternity inside the mind of the Maker. In the solitude of that infinite mind, we encounter the ultimate reality and the love responsible for all things.

In the vastness of the mind of God we discover the characters and plot setting the stage for the coming world drama. In her book *The Mind of the Maker*, Dorothy Sayers draws an intriguing parallel between the Trinity and the development of a book. Every book, she says, begins in the mind of its creator. The setting, characters and story line are creations formed in the thoughts of the writer. Those ideas eventually are transformed into words, which form the content of a book one day to be read by the reader.

In the shadows of eternity, an awesome idea for a really great story was being developed. Before there was time, before there was space, when God was all that existed, a brilliant plot was wrapping itself around a grace-full idea. These passionate ideas and plans were being formed in the mind of the Creator and cast a shadow over all His beloved creation: *the shadow of His presence.*

The imaginations creating the story were in harmony with the love flowing out of Father's heart. Stimulating the thinking in His mind were the powerful passions stirring in His heart. The thoughts in His mind were eventually translated into words—words that would form the outline of an incredible plan. In the beginning, the Scriptures tell us, was the Word. The Word was the full expression of the thoughts of this magnificent Maker. But before a word could exist, there had to be thoughts, conceived from an inspired idea.

Divine deliberations, timeless thoughts, creative concepts, and powerful plans were assembling themselves into an amazing arrangement of literary genius. The ideas stretching forth from His mind longed for their moment of unveiling. By the way, each one of us was there in those thoughts. Time was there. A whole brand-new world was waiting to burst forth from the mind of a wonderful Maker.

> First, there is the Creative Idea, passionless, timeless, beholding the whole work complete at once, the end in the beginning; and this is the image of the Father.[3]
>
> Dorothy L. Sayers

Whatever God thinks, is. Father has the power to transform thought into visible reality. His thoughts were gathering themselves together in an orderly and passionate form, ready to be displayed in a glorious manifestation of heavenly magnitude: *all made possible by the Image-Maker.*

The divine idea was magnificent in the breadth of its detail and yet so intimate in the passion of its purpose. Before the divine purpose was manifested in creation it was first conceived in the mind of the Maker. Only a God of love could conceive of a plan so wonderful, so beautiful, and yet so mysterious.

The Plan in the Mind of the Maker

The Creator's heart pounded with delight as He considered the possibilities of His inspired idea. His thought was to create a being in His own image with whom He could share His love and His throne. At this point it is important to understand the context of the word "love." As we will explore later, one of the great challenges of modern Christianity is to provide meaning to the words religion uses in the descriptions of spiritual realities. Too often we are guilty of using buzzwords and trite clichés that fail to connect with the deepest parts of our being.

God's love for man is not a meaningless cliché. It is lavishly rich in content expressing itself in actions on behalf of His beloved children. God's thoughts concerning you are saturated with extravagant emotions of desire and devotion. Thinking about you put a smile on His face. He longs for the presence of your company. He is devoted to your well-being. You are the focus of His unlimited affection as He is constantly calling you from the depths of your being. He really, really likes you.

Too often this divine love-call is silenced by the other voices screaming for attention in our daily, self-absorbed thoughts. The sounds of shame, rejection and judgment are alien voices, the voices of dark strangers. Unfortunately, the sounds of sweet nothings being whispered in your ears by your loving Father fail to reach you due to the relentless noise of negative thinking. The ancient language of Eden is infused with terms of endearment flowing from the heart of Father. These are the lost words that were replaced with the words of a guilt-ridden religion.

Because God intimately desired to "give" Himself to you, He took of His own nature and fashioned a creature just like Him. This being was to be the focus of the warmth of His love. Together they would enjoy each other's presence as they freely and openly expressed the passions of their hearts. The created one would never know loneliness or fear because the Creator would always be there to caress and comfort him. God smiled as He pensively considered the plan.

In the core of the plan you are there in the heart and mind of the Creator. Since the beginning of time you have been in His heart and on His mind. Who you are stretches backward in time, right to the very beginning. You were there in eternity, in the heart and mind of the Maker. You are neither the result of an impulsive moment nor the conjecture of a careless creator. You are a thoughtfully inspired image formed in His loving thoughts. No matter the circumstances of your birth, your origin is in God. You are a product of a God who loves you and desires only the very best for your life.

In order for the Creator and the creature to have a place to enjoy each other's presence, a world was created. This world was to be the setting for a free expression of the love and creativity flowing from one to the other. The artistry creating this environment is a compelling manifestation of the mind of a wise and loving God. The passion He felt in His heart would soon be expressed in what He was to make through His Word.

The greater the mind, the greater the possibility for an elaborate and extravagant creation. The more complex the creation, the greater the potential for problems, for a breakdown in the final plan. In forming a creature who was free to chose his own destiny, Father was taking a great risk. But the risk was worth the possibilities of the love that gave birth to that freedom.

The greater the heart, the more loving and gracious are the contingencies created for the potential disruptions in the divine purpose. Any interference in the fulfillment of the dream of the Creator for His created one would have to be countered. All divine counter-actions would be inspired and initiated by the powerful compassion driving His heart.

A Loving Heart Brings Forth a Master Plan

Love was the lining of the womb in which the plan was conceived. Even the most seemingly insignificant portion of the creation was designed with careful precision and put in place by His extravagant love. Though the environment in which the creature lives seems to sometimes mask the love of the Maker, the love is always there. It will not be shaken. It will not be offended. It will not be blocked. The love that created the plan is always pursuing the objects of that plan.

The merciful Master painted all of creation with a brush of inspired love. Passion gave birth to the plan, and love was the logic behind the purposes of God. All of the carefully crafted creation testifies to the brilliance of the logic displayed in that amazing love. Love was the push that gave birth to creation.

The Power of the Word

Words are powerful forces creating either positive or negative energy. The things we speak have the power to encourage others and create comfort in the heart of the hearer. But they also have the power to tear down and damage the human spirit when spoken out of the darkness of our hearts. The spirit and the content of our words determine their effect upon our world.

God, who is love, speaks words that create life, hope and comfort. The words of the Creator flow out of the boundless love in His heart and bring forth a marvelous world. The world created by the

Word was to be a place where man could passionately experience a living relationship with a loving God.

In the beginning was the Word, and the Word was with God, and the Word was God. He was in the beginning with God All things came into being by Him, and apart from Him nothing came into being that has come into being.   John 1:1-3

The words spoken from the mouth of God resulted in new worlds materializing into new vistas of living, visual reality. The Word entered the darkness of nonbeing, creating life and new dimensions of truth. The Master of the ancient language said the words He speaks are spirit and life (see John 6:63). As the Word entered the darkness of our inner life, it formed waves of inspired light, enabling a peek into the spiritual dimension of truth and reality.

Before there was faith, there was the Word. Faith cannot exist without the Word. The Word gives power to our faith. In the beginning the power of the Word brought forth a world of living things. The Word eternally stands alone as primal, virginal power creating and sustaining worlds within worlds.

Faith is dependent on the articulated word. By itself it has no power. The hearing of the Word energizes it. Without words there can be no faith. Faith needs a focus. The voice of God is that focus. The Voice stimulates the spirit, creating the response we call faith.

That voice is indispensable to the true operation of faith. The cripple will remain at the pool of Bethesda unless the Voice is heard. The demoniac continues to roam the mountainside, tormented by evil spirits, until the Voice roars forth from the mouth of the approaching God. The adulteress remains in her bondage to sin at the mercy of spiteful religious men until the Word exposes their own sin and sets her free. The Word exposes us so that He can heal us.

In an effort to help men understand this spiritual law, Jesus spoke these words: "Everyone who hears these words of Mine, and acts upon them, may be compared to a wise man, who built his house upon the rock" (see Luke 6:47).

"Hears these words"—the utterance of God's Word is the starting point for faith. "Acts upon them"—faith is the attitude created by the spoken word. Faith is the spiritual energy released by the words of God. To act without the Voice is to take a false step of pre-sumption, for true faith flows from the fountain of the spoken word.

In the beginning God created...
In the beginning was the Word...

From the mind of the Maker the word, first powerfully formed, was lovingly spoken. At the sounding of that Word, time is born, and a world is created. The Word passed through the gates of eternity and, bursting forth, began to create. In those first ticking moments of time, an environment was fashioned for the creative action of the Word.

The space of our surroundings and the essence of our existence were created by the imaginations of God. What the Maker imagined in His mind, the Word brought into existence. A word cannot exist without a thought. But a thought is nothing until it is manifested as a word.

The moment had come. One act of creation led to yet another. The Spirit moved over the face of the dark world as it prepared the environment for the spoken Word. The Creator released the Word. The Word moved as an unstoppable creative force in the darkness of disorder. Systematically, lovingly, and with great accuracy each part was created and positioned in its appropriate place.

There was no hurry. Eternity, not time, was controlling the mo-ment. Everything was being created in agreement with the Image of the Maker. The Word was fixed at the core of creation and was the center around which all of creation spun in orchestrated motion. Everything was created in relationship to Him.

The Creation of Man

A world had been created, a world teeming with embryonic life. Everything was now ready for the culminating piece of the Master's touch–the creation of man. Without this final part the plan would be incomplete, the story unfinished. God formed the world in His imaginings. These thoughts became an image. In the likeness of that Image other images would be created. And God would love the image and say it is good. These extraordinary images, called hu-mans, would each be unique in their own physical representation of the creative Word.

The time arrived for the creation of the creature. The Image-Maker gazed intently upon the human, recently formed by the power of His creative thoughts and the workmanship of His loving hands. Thoughtfully, He pictured the possibilities of the life they might enjoy together. With eyes reflecting desire and compassion, He gazed deeply into man's lifeless and hollow eyes. In that moment the eternal plan reached its highest stage.

The Image-Maker made a move toward the creature. Man had been there in His thoughts, it seemed forever, and now he would stand before Him as a living being, image of His Image, creation of His love. Father could hardly wait to hold him in His arms.

A Kiss From the Father

Compelled by the intense longing to experience Himself, Father placed His lips on the face of man. As the warmth of Divine compassion pressed lovingly against the human vessel, God gathered Himself for the moment He had so long anticipated.

Breathing in deeply and with one great force of spirit-wind, a surge of divine breath exploded, as it were from His mouth, instantly filling every portion of the creature's being. As celestial substance poured into the creature lying still in Creator's arms, and the first of a new species came into being.

In that instant, divine life infused the lifeless matter held in the arms of the Creator. The final result was almost instantaneous. Out of the dark shadows of nonbeing, a life came forth, and a spirit was created.

Man arose out of the darkness of nonbeing into the majestic light of being when the powerful celestial substance filled his life. If the breath of spirit-wind were ever extinguished, man would return to nonbeing. It is his life. This celestial matter was the power that would enable him to utter the first words of the ancient language.

Man was born into the world that had lived in the mind of the Maker. As man opened his eyes, he looked steadfastly into the face of God. The presence of God was man's original environment. In that presence man will always know life and love. Glory, which is the mask of God's presence, was the environment in which man was created. Man would always crave the presence, even when it would be obscured by man's dark environment.

Man was born in the intimacy of a creative and loving moment. With the light of eternity shining on his face, man looked into the "face of God." It was a face of love and desire that awakened man that day. Man was immediately captivated by the wonderful mystery of that love, which would pursue him all the days of his life.

The Image of God

The very life of man is a bit of God. Man is of the essence of God. Every man is the presence-chamber of God.[4]

S.D. Gordon

It took two independent ingredients to bring life to man—body and spirit. As spirit was breathed into man's body he came to life. The soul was the consequential product of man's body coming into contact with the Spirit of the living God. The soul, with its mind, will and emotions, is the image of God.

The breath of God was the catalyst for the creation of man. This celestial substance gave life, enabling man to live in a new dimension. It opened the door for man to be transported into the realm of God. In this dimension called spirit, man would communicate and know fellowship with the Image-Maker.

Without the spirit, the life of the soul is diminished as it sinks into darkness. As long as man's spirit is alive, he could live above the natural realm and soar into spiritual realms and fellowship with his Creator. This is what sets man apart from the rest of creation. The image of the Creator was massaged into the DNA of the created being, making him unique among all God's creation. The image of God in man, in the living soul, sets him apart. Man alone is a being full of spiritual inspiration, not animal instinct.

Created to be a Creator

God was inspired with an idea. God then breathed into man. He in-spired man, and man lived by the strength of that inspiration. Man's ability to think, speak, reason, plan, create, imagine, build, feel, love—these are the things that set him apart.

God placed Adam in a world where he would be inspired to create just like his Creator. Man's imaginings would create other worlds that would give glory to the great Creator. As long as God was the source of inspiration, then man would be able to continue reasoning and creating new worlds that would bring pleasure to the Creator.

God also gave man a freedom in which to create. This freedom is critical to the plan. It is in the environment of freedom that creativity expresses itself best. If freedom is repressed, then creativity suffers. Unfortunately the church has not always understood this eternal principle.

The creativity of man could be freely manifested in loving response to the Creator. The divine inspirations would enable him to build for Father's glory. This is what the Image-Maker desired—to see the sons of His love responding in worshipful acts of passion toward the Creator and in creative acts of compassion for his neighbor.

God also gave man a conscience as a rudder for those creative actions. The conscience would direct him toward the Father and inspire him in his love for man. It would stimulate him and motivate him upward in his desire to be like his Creator.

Spirit, Soul and Body

Man was created as spirit having a soul journeying through the dimension of time in a vehicle called a body. The spirit is able to communicate with the world through the body. The soul lies in between these two worlds. It can communicate with God through the spirit and can communicate with the world through the body. The soul has the power of self-determination. It can make decisions concerning the things in its environment, accepting or rejecting them and relating to them or withdrawing from them.

The body communicated with the material world and is the lowest. It is a created vessel for our journey in time. Between the spirit and the body is the soul. The function of the soul is to maintain the spirit and the body in their proper order. It is the fulcrum point, the balance that creates perfect harmony between the spirit and the body.

> The soul looks to the spirit for supply received which the latter has and communicates to the body what it has received so that the body can partake of the perfection of the Holy Spirit and become a spiritual body.[5]
>
> Watchman Nee

The soul must remain subservient to the spirit. As it does, it can issue spiritually inspired commands to the body and all will remain in perfect harmony with the will of the Image-Maker. There is a synergy of synchronous movement between each part of man. The life of God resident in the spirit of man finds no obstruction as it flows through the soul and is physically manifested in the actions of man, walking in fellowship with his God, obeying His every word. Thus the soul could also help him avoid the darkness created by self-will.

Created in the image of God, man could now arise from the earthen bed and carry out the plan of Father-Creator. Man was created for purpose. The mystery of the proposed plan was waiting for man's discovery.

The Discovery of the Plan

As we have just seen, the thought became an idea, the idea was expressed in the Word, and the image in man became the vessel for the plan. There in the beginning of time, in the primitive garden, we discover the original plan, enabling us to understand our life and destiny. The plan enveloped in the mind of the Image-Maker has left its deep impressions on us. We cannot escape it no matter how hard we sometimes try. The plan is carefully constructed, but is fluid and flexible, not fixed and rigid. It is important to understand this truth. The plan adapts itself to the environment and to the individual created for the execution of the divine strategy.

Never forget that the plan is simple. God desired to have one like Himself in order to share with him the great mysteries of eternity. His desire is to have a relationship with man. He pursued the sharing together of a life and a purpose. He longs for a connection, a bonding, a rapport—a relationship with another being like unto Himself.

God created the environment as the backdrop for this loving relationship. God is love. For love to exist there must be a focus for that love. Love that is simply a concept is not love. Love must find a way to demonstrate its passion. Man is the focus of that search.

God's great desire was to experience the power of that love in a living relationship with His creation. His yearning was that the enthusiasm and force of that love would be received by His creation in a mutually loving relationship. The plan began in a love relationship with Adam and Eve and was to extend itself throughout time to every living being and thus "fill" the whole earth with Himself.

The End Continually Seeks the Beginning

The original plan made clear in the beginning has been lost to man. Man complicated the simple plan with the interjection of his own thoughts and plans. The challenge of rediscovering the mystery of the plan is enormous.

Man is conditioned in his thinking process to reason along certain fixed paths. These paths are the worn trails of traveled truth that make it difficult for us to think outside the box of religious rationalizations. It is difficult for man to break off from this path.

Unfortunately, many have lost touch with the reality in which our world began. Time has worn away the edges of our memory of the divine strategy and has reshaped it into a distorted religious reality. This religious reality casts a dark, gross shadow over God's world, obscuring His ultimate purpose and desires. Few have been able to escape the treacherous hold of religious thought. The only way to escape is to find our way back to the beginning.

Jacob Boehme, the German mystic, describes a concept called the "circular process." In this mystical process, he declares, "The end continually seeks the beginning."

Man is a wanderer. In the progression of civilization man is inclined to move away from the wonder of the original moment. All of life moves from the simple to the complex. Sometimes this growth is good, and sometimes it is bad. It is a tragedy when we migrate from the innocence experienced in the beginning of our relationship with God, drifting toward the complications developed in the process of "spiritual growth."

A little seed grows into the intricacies of a beautiful tree. A young child grows from the innocence of its beginning into the sophistication and struggles of an adult life. The church emerges out of the simplicity of its humble beginnings and is transformed into a complex system of religious order. The Protestant Reformation begins in purity as it breaks free from a legalistic system. However, it quickly evolves into its own complicated, restricted and religious order.

All of life moves toward deterioration and descent into the darkness of a matrix restricting freedom and creativity, the things making the human unique. Man has a propensity to get lost in the very things he constructs, and this principle certainly includes the church. It is sad to view the swamp created by religious thought, which man must trample through on his journey toward God.

Man's deep sense of loneliness is a testimony to the fact that he has lost his way. He is detached from his original environment and thus isolated from the divine purpose. Religion is a poor substitute for God's plan and only contributes to the cloud of unknowing.

Man has complicated the plan with so much religious speech and veiled the wonder of its original configuration. We have convoluted the plan with a system that does not allow man the freedom to find his way home. We have covered the path with our selfish ideas, authoritarian rule and legalistic systems. Religion posts itself at the gate of the ancient garden insisting that man perform his religious duty in order to enter in.

I Want to Go 'Home'

Within the concept of the circular process is another force equally as strong as this law of detachment and deterioration. Some simplistically call it "nostalgia." Others call it "homesickness." Nostalgia is a powerful inner force subjectively reminding us of a better day and simpler times. All of us, at one time or another, have felt its powerful draw.

> Why is it that one can never think of the past without wanting to go back?[6]   C.S. Lewis

The power of "nostalgia" jogs our memories, making us reminiscent of our beginning, calling us back to the original matrix of creation, the beginning of all things. This *heavenly homesickness* is also another gift from the Creator. It is like an internal alarm clock, and when it sounds it awakens us and reminds us it is time to arise and return home to Father. The restlessness we sense when we have lost the way is a spiritual mechanism placed inside of us by Father-Creator. It is a human love-call bidding us to come home.

It is often accompanied by a sense of discontent, restlessness and emptiness. The Creator has worked this psychological feeling into the essence of our being. Seventeenth century French philosopher Blaise Paschal described man as being created with an inner void and declared that this void can only be filled with God. The influence of this inner void overwhelms us at times, as we become prey to its constant reminder that we were created for something "larger than ourselves." When it begins its magical work within us we cannot shake it. Ignoring it will only bring further frustration. It will only subside when we give in and start the journey back home, back to the ancient garden.

Any attempt to fill it with another substance or other pursuits, even religious stuff, will not work. God has placed eternity in our hearts and there is no joy, no belonging, and no fulfillment until we find our way back to our beginning.

Beginnings of a New Language

This plan was the topic of discussion between God and man in the garden. The passion of the plan filled their conversation. These intimate conversations became the first syllables uttered by man and slowly developed into a language. Every day Father-Creator chose new words to express to the human the definition and scope of this glorious plan. Adam had many questions, and Father patiently answered the probing questions. These conversations spoken in the sacred setting of Eden were the formative stages of the evolving ancient language of Eden. To discover the dialect of the ancient language of Eden we must return to the primitive garden.

> God created man in his own image and likeness, i.e. made him a creator too, calling him to free spontaneous activity and not to formal obedience to His power. Free creativeness is the creature's answer to the great call of its creator. Man's creative work is the fulfillment of the Creator's secret will.[7]   Nicolas Berdyaev

Endnotes

1. *Collected Poems*, T.S. Eliot, Harcourt Brace and Company, New York, 1962, p. 81, 82.

2. *Centuries of Meditation*, Traherne, www.ccel.org/ccel/traherne/centuries.v.html.

3. *The Mind of the Maker*, Dorothy L. Sayers, Harper and Row, New York, New York, 1941, p. 37.

4. *Quiet Talks About Jesus*, S.D. Gordon, Destiny Image Publishers, Shippensburg, Pennsylvania, 2003, p. 15.

5. *The Spiritual Man, Vol. 1*, Watchman Nee, Living Streams Ministry, 1992, p. 9.

6. *The Quotable Lewis*, Wayne Martindale and Jerry Root, Tyndale House Publishers, Wheaton, Illinois, 1989, p. 423.

7. *The Mind of the Maker*, Dorothy L. Sayers, p. 61 (Berdyaev: *The Destiny of Man*).

How like an angel came I down!
How bright are all things here!
When first among his works I did appear
O how their glory me did crown!
The world resembled his eternity,
In which my soul did walk;
And ev'ry thing that I did see
Did with me talk[1]

Thomas Traherne

CHAPTER 3

A LANGUAGE IS BORN IN EDEN

The heavens are telling of the glory of God; and their ex-
panse is declaring the work of His hand.   Psalm 19:1

The earth is the Lord's and all its fullness. Everywhere man
looks he can see the splendor of this wondrous setting created by Father for the objects of His love. In the great expanses of the universe,
Earth is unequaled in its uniqueness in creation. Hidden everywhere
in this sacred universe are embedded codes and symbolic signs testifying to the existence and creativity of the Creator and His love for
humankind. My dad called this "imprisoned splendor."

For those who have eyes to see, the earth contains a hidden dialect reflective of the heavenly language. In its own way it declares
the loving care of the Father. Those who seek to transcend the casu-
al look at nature to contemplate the wonders of the world may discover the secret keys. As an example, Father fixed the sun in the
middle of man's universe reminding him that in His world all things
revolve around the Son—who is the outshining of the Father.

The constancy of the times and seasons are a daily reminder of
His faithfulness. As sure as the revolving seasons, so certain is Father's love. To forever remind man that the light of His wonderful
presence always follows the "dark night of the soul," God caused
first the evening and then the morning to make a day. The evening
night is always followed by the morning light.

Weeping may last for the night, but a shout of joy comes
in the morning.   Psalm 30:5

These covert codes, if perceived by the spirit, would enhance
man's ability to speak the ancient language, encouraging him in
his own journey and providing inspired encouragement to his fellow sojourners.

Your lovingkindness, O Lord, extends to the heavens,
Your faithfulness reaches to the skies.
Your righteousness is like the mountains of God;
Your justice is like a great deep.   Psalm 36:5-6

Jesus, the restorer of the ancient language, was a master at unlocking nature's codes and revealing the mysteries of the life and love of the Father. The parables of Jesus are full of keys to help us understand the mysterious wonders in the universe. Jesus used the realities of the natural world of man to reveal the realities of the spiritual world of Father. Those who had ears to hear were able to unlock the wisdom found in His words.

First Lessons in the Ancient Language of Eden

The earth was created as a special place for the manifestation of God's love and the outworking of His plans. In this hallowed location, Father commenced man's first lessons in the ancient language. The gracious plans of Father were the textbook used for teaching man the native tongue; the Garden of Eden was the classroom where man began his first lessons.

We must continually refer back to that plan because it is the golden thread running through history. It is too easy to lose sight of the plan and God's commitment to its fulfillment. If repetition is the mother of learning, we must continually be reminded of the original blueprints drawn by the Master's hands. Starting with God's desire for a human relationship, the strategy culminated in a being created in His image to be the object of His desire. Only a being created in His image could experience a relationship with God. So man is the focal point of the Image-Maker's designs. In this loving relationship is found the roots of the mother tongue of Eden.

The happiness which God designs for His higher creatures
of being freely, voluntarily united to Him and to each
other is an ecstasy of love and delight.[2]   C.S. Lewis

It was Father's desire that man, in turn, would generate that image in others. Hearing love-words spoken softly in his soul by Father, man would find within himself new words to express the marvel of their intimate relationship. Those creative words would form new worlds of human relationships reflective of His love. Grace and mercy are the key demonstrative nouns of the primitive language. The language of Eden is not the dead language of religion, satisfied only with theological explanations. The vocabulary of the garden expressed itself in the spiritual encounters with Father. The plan was simple.

Unfortunately, this simple plan quickly began to fade into obscurity as it was replaced by man's substitute strategies arising out of his insecurities and lust. Man seeks ways to dominate others rather than serving them, to take from others rather than giving, to damage others rather than saving, to restrict creativity rather than enhancing originality, and to place himself before others rather than considering them better than himself. Any deviation from Father's plan will create a disturbance in the universe, disrupting the Father's intentions and causing the language of Eden to diminish.

In the beginning it was not so. If man is to be freed from the bondage created by his own selfish ambitions, he must find his way back to the beginning—to a garden created by the Father for His lovingly created Son. In that garden, at the edge of time, is where we will discover man's original environment and his native tongue, the ancient language of Eden. The end is found in the beginning.

Eden—The Garden of God

The Lord God planted a garden toward the east, in Eden; and there He placed the man whom He had formed.

Genesis 2:8

God made man and immediately gave him a home, mankind's first home. God called this home the Garden of Eden, a place uniquely formed for the son of His love. Giving special and loving regard to the formation of this perfect setting for Adam, it would be the model for all future homes—furnished with love, freedom, acceptance, creativity, companionship and peace. This model home would eventually become many homes in which the ancient language would be spoken. Many homes would become nations, and these nations were to reflect the glory of that first home. What a wonderful plan!

A Garden in the East

The Bible says the Garden of Eden was planted "eastward." We're not told what the garden was eastward of, but the Bible commonly uses the word "east" in connection with Jesus.

And behold, the glory of the God of Israel was coming from the way of the east. And His voice was like the sound of many waters; and the earth shone with His glory.
                                                            Ezekiel 43:2

"Where is He who has been born King of the Jews? For we saw His star in the east and have come to worship Him.
                                                            Matthew 2:2

"For just as the lightning comes from the east and flashes even to the west, so will the coming of the Son of Man be."
                                                            Matthew 24:27

The Lord is "a sun and shield" (Psalm 84:11), and for those who fear Him, "the sun of righteousness will rise with healing in its wings" (Malachi 4:2). He is the rising Sun coming from the East. No matter where you are, the sun always rises in the east, bringing its brilliant light and comforting warmth. So it is with the Son of man.

Ezekiel says that the Prince will come through the eastern gate (Ezekiel 43:1-4); and the wise men saw His star in the east (Matthew 2:2). The Garden of Eden, typifying the Kingdom of God, the home of man, was planted eastward. When man looks to the rising sun he is unconsciously reminded of his original home and the native language he once spoke.

There is something in the heart of God that is drawn to the East. I do not understand the full implications of this truth, but I sense that its reality has special significance. It is a mystery with prophetic meaning that will be unlocked in His time. I do know that all mysteries are locked up in the person of Jesus. The greater the unveiling of Christ, the greater our understanding of the mysteries of the ages. It is, I am convinced, a waste of time to try and understand the mysteries of God before we have discovered the Son of God. He is our guide into the spiritual realms, where all things are revealed.

Eden was a unique habitat for the newly created creature. Adam grew and prospered in the benevolent presence of Father. The presence was the very air he breathed. In this magnificent environment man could mature into the fullness of His beloved Creator's image. Father had a son in whom He could delight, the son of His love, the object of His total affection, and the garden was their special meeting place.

The Birthplace of Delight and Desire

Beauty is in the eye of the beholder, so God gave man eyes to behold the splendor of His creative work. Beholding the beauty of His handiwork causes the heart to worship. Eyes that do not see the beauty of God's world are unable to appreciate the wonder of His word and cannot ascend into the high places of worship. The beauty of God's world inspired Adam to create his own melody of thanksgiving.

Desire also was born in the Garden of Eden. Springing from the delight experienced in the garden, spiritual yearnings poured forth from the heart of man. We desire what brings us delight. When man awoke, the first thing his eyes beheld was the face of God, and desire immediately welled up within him—desire to live his life in a relationship with this wondrous Being, to know His ways, to be with Him, and to please Him.

The day desire was born language came into being. Man's desire began to search for ways to convey its excitement. Adam could not silently contain the desires of his heart. They had to be spoken. His desire to communicate his delight in the Father necessitated words. Tentatively, he began to speak, and soon the words he sought poured forth. Man was overflowing with desire—a desire for God and a passion to articulate the intense feelings of his heart. His walks with God in the primitive garden were the occasion for the first expressions of the language of Eden.

The Dancing God and the Ancient Language

The biblical descriptions of life in Eden are enough to give a sense of the beauty of the garden sanctuary and the loving relationship between Adam and Father. But it is not fully detailed in its descriptions. Based upon the limited information available, I have drawn upon my own imagination to describe the wonder of that loving relationship between Adam and his beloved Father.

Adam delighted in the presence of Father. Their daily walks together were occasions of profound joy and pleasure. Father was deeply pleased with the object of His creation. Adam was everything

He had ever hoped for. He had never known such joy. Their hearts overflowed with love for each other.

As God observed Adam's playful activity in the land of Eden, He could not resist the ecstasy erupting in His heart. His was a father's pride in his son. Adam was such a delight. Adam's innocence, his childlike spirit, his desire to be with Father—all these things filled God's heart with such unbelievable joy.

As that joy bubbled up within Him, Father could feel the heavenly harmonies beginning to well up inside Him. I can imagine Him pulling up the "skirts of His royal robe" (Psalm 133:2) as His feet began to tap in delightful synchronization to a melody only He could hear. Beset with divine ecstasy Father just had to dance. Spinning and twirling, laughing and shouting, Father gave vent to the deeply satisfying love He experienced in the presence of Adam.

> *"The Lord your God is in your midst, a victorious warrior. He will exult over you with joy, He will be quiet in His love, He will rejoice over you with shouts of joy."*
>   Zephaniah 3:17

Adam loved the dance and laughed in great delight. As he watched Father's antics he was overcome with pure pleasure and joy. I believe this was the day music was born in the earth regions, as Father danced in the presence of Adam. He prayed these days would never end.

As Adam looked at the face of Father and at the world Father had created for him, a vocabulary of heavenly language was beginning to form in his spirit—words of love and worship. The first words spoken by man harmonized with the words originally spoken by his Father. As man contemplated his world he looked into Father's eyes and said, "It is good." And God smiled.

Man would often share his gratefulness to his Father for the wonderful world given to him. Adam deeply desired to be a meaningful part of His unique plan. The articulations of his heart reflected his desire to be one with His God. The accent and developing idioms were animated by the deep awe inspired by the passion and plan of Father.

The Sounds of Silence

In those days of loving courtship man lived for his daily walks with God when they leisurely moved toward their favorite places in the Garden. Eden was like an old love shack set in the middle of Father's universe. How Adam loved that place! It was in those trying times that his language took on form and substance. He reached deep into his within for the things stirring in his heart and the questions forming in his mind.

He somehow knew he could speak with absolutely no fear of saying or asking the wrong thing. There were no restrictions imposed on him. No fear of crossing the line. No fear of offending or being misunderstood. This total freedom of speech allowed him to explore all the emerging feelings in his heart. He searched for and found the words. There seemed to be no end to them, and God was pleased.

This evolving language contained passionate words, yet at the same time it created such an atmosphere of trust that words were not even needed. Adam could feel God's love even when words were not spoken. I have learned that sometimes to speak a word destroys the majesty of a moment. The sounds of silence can be so powerful. Adam felt in perfect harmony with Father even in those moments of pregnant silence. At times they just stood there simply enjoying each other's presence.

Father's very presence had a mysterious way of communicating His love, leaving a deep impression upon Adam's soul. Man was learning not just the spoken word, but also the silent language of the heart perfectly attuned to its Creator. Busy about some task, he would inexplicably become aware of the Presence gently making itself felt in his spirit. He would often sense that presence impinging on the skirts of his being. Sadly, man would lose this spiritual capacity to recognize his Maker in the sounds of silence as the Presence would draw near.

God is love, and that love is God's fundamental expression toward man. He comes speaking a silent language understood in an inner awakening, a realization. Words fail to effectively describe the place we may find ourselves by carefully attuning our spirits to His. Adam was born attuned to God—his spirit was allowing him to hear the ancient language even when his ears heard no sound. *Father was and is always speaking, even in the sounds of silence.*

Language—A Mirror of the Soul

In the developing language of Adam, every word was a reflection of an inward reality—a total harmony between the spoken word and the inner thought. Just as parents can understand their young child's first mostly incoherent words, so God understood each newly articulated word of His beloved man. While his first utterances were few and simple, man grew in his capacity to explore and express his thoughts and feelings, becoming more creative in his attempts to communicate his heart. Father was delighted with each new step Adam took in his deepening awareness of himself and his relation to Father's created world.

As the words Father spoke entered man's spirit, they illuminated directly, immediately, and intimately. The spirit of man was innocent and clear, allowing the divine words to be received undiluted by *knowledge*, and were assimilated into the soul of man. As Father's words entered the heart of man, they created within him new phrases that could accurately describe the spiritual reality encompassing him.

In the Garden of Eden, there was a perfect "goodness of fit." The symbols of speech perfectly reflected the image of the soul. The words exchanged between the Creator and the creature thoroughly manifested the feelings in their hearts—with neither confusion nor ambiguity. There were no types and no shadows, only a certainty of communication, each clearly understanding the other.

> Human consciousness lies between two abysses, the upper and the lower, the superconsciousness and the consciousness. Moral consciousness which formulates laws and norms comes up both against the instinctive, subconscious, primeval nature and against grace, superconsciousness and the divine.[3]   Nicolas Berdyaev

There was no spiritual conflict in the consciousness of man. No homespun morality clouded the consciousness of his thought life. Thoughts of what was right and what was wrong were not playing on the strings of his thinking process. His inner life was filled with the power of spiritual light and divine grace, creating an environment of grace in which he was free to speak his heart. The inner environs of his soul—filled with the light of uninhibited love—enabled him to freely and creatively express the affections of his heart.

Language was the means of revealing the thoughts of Adam's heart—a mirror of his soul. There was no shame or guilt on the path that man and God traveled together. There was no psychoanalyzing each other's words. There was no hidden language, no coded speech. Father was discovering new delights in the expressions of Adam's heart, and Adam was learning the fathomless depth of Father's love for him. The heart-to-heart give-and-take blended into a melody of inexpressible beauty.

Eden—A Place of Creativity

Then the Lord God took the man and put him into the Garden of Eden to cultivate it and keep it. Genesis 2:15

God created man in his own image and likeness, i.e. made him a creator too, calling him to free spontaneous activity and not to formal obedience to His power. Free creativeness is the creature's answer to the great call of its creator. Man's creative work is the fulfillment of the Creator's secret will.[4]   Nicolas Berdyaev

The garden created by the Father was placed under the custodial care of Adam. God placed Adam in the garden to be a creator just like Father. Work was a part of God's original purpose for man, but there was a perfect order to that work. If the order were violated it would disturb the inner peace of man and have disastrous consequences.

This was the order: God worked and then He rested, and man begins his work in the realm of Father's rest. Man's first day begins in the rest of God. In that rest he, too, is able to work effectively and creatively. Man must never violate this arrangement. If he does not do his work in the rest of God, then creativity is adversely affected, peace is disrupted, and man's work turns into sweat. There was no sweat in the garden.

God's world was the source of Adam's creative work in the garden. Man was created to become a creator like his Maker. He would express that creative ability by nurturing the world given to him by

Father. Man did not have the ability to create from nothingness like his Father, but he was given a mind and a heart to create powerful and wonderful things from the material supplied by the Creator.

Father created a world of matter that would be the material for man's creative work. Man's creativity was expressed in the manner in which he rearranged and joined together the natural elements of his Father's world. Man's creative work was a form of worship.

Work performed in the dimension of divine rest would always be a source of fulfillment and satisfaction for man. It would not be a forced labor, but a spontaneous and free response to the will of the Father. Only the labor camps of religion could destroy the creative work of man. Man's creative work established a new forum for the conversations between man and His Creator. His activity in the garden was a source of great joy for Father. Overwhelmed by the joys of his labor Adam would chatter away with Father as he jubilantly described every new detail of his creative work. And Father smiled.

The freedom Father had given Adam was a key to the artistic work. An original, inspired work always includes the factor of freedom. Freedom of expression is central to the creative part of man. God put Adam in the garden and gave him a unique purpose: tend and cultivate. Father did not tell Adam how, when or where. He was not placed in a sphere of heavy rules and regulations. He was given the power of purpose and the gift of freedom to express that purpose through his own work. Empowered with purpose he was left to freely create within the circle of the divine intention. Adam's work was a part of the ancient language because his work was a creative communication of his internal inspirations.

Man's creative work is a spiritual sign of his answer to the call of God and participation in the work of God. Poet T.S. Eliot put it this way: "The Lord who created must wish us to create and employ our creation again in His service."[5] Adam experienced a sense of fulfillment as he learned to harmonize his work with Father's purposes. His work spoke for itself.

Father looked upon the work of man and said, "It is good." And man smiled.

Eden—A Place of Community

Then the Lord God said, "It is not good for the man to be alone; I will make him a helper suitable for him."

Genesis 2:18

In those early days in the garden, God paraded all kinds of birds and animals before Adam, giving him the task of naming each one. As Adam fixed his gaze upon each animal he searched his thoughts for the appropriate name that would identify each species among God's creation. For a while this activity served as a distraction from a growing loneliness. None of the animals would ever be a suitable companion for Adam. By the time Adam had finished naming all the animals the sense of loneliness had reached an unhealthy proportion. Everything in the garden was just right for Adam except one thing: He had no suitable companion for himself. A longing for human companionship was taking shape deep within him.

God understood the seclusion in which Adam was fixed and perceived the psychological consequences. There was no creature on earth just like him. God realized it was not good for Adam to be alone, so He acted. God always responds passionately to the needs of His beloved creature. Father is always moved to divine action by the sorrow flowing from man's troubles. There is always a divine response to the human predicament.

God put Adam into a deep sleep. Sleep was designed as a temporary break from man's afflictions. While man rested God went to work. What a powerful truth!

While he was sleeping God took a piece of bone out of Adam's side. From this portion of man God created a companion. As the spiritual anesthesia wore off Adam looked around for Father. Slowly in the distance he saw Father as He walked down the aisle of Eden bringing a creature with Him. Standing before Adam, Father lifted the veil over woman and presented her to Adam.

God looked deeply into Adam's eyes waiting to see his reaction. Father was curious to see how man might respond to His creation. God was not disappointed by Adam's response. Adam smiled and said, "Thank you, Father."

To Adam, the woman was the most beautiful creature he had ever seen. He was permeated with pleasure as he prophetically proclaimed, "This is now bone of my bones, and flesh of my flesh" (Genesis 2:23). Adam had enjoyed the presence of the animal world surrounding him in Father's garden, but this gift from Father was greater than any other creation.

Man was delighted with God's gift, and the thanksgiving directed toward God was another early expression of spiritual worship—
a thankful heart for God's gifts. The woman Father created for
Adam pleased him greatly for she was matched perfectly to him.
This first human relationship would be the beginning of all human
relationships. The pleasure and security they enjoyed in the presence of each other would be the foundation for the future communities of man.

The First Human Community

The man and the woman were very happy in the Garden of
Eden. They became husband and wife in a marriage performed by
Father. Now everything was perfect. Adam had the companion his
heart had longed for. He no doubt told her of all his experiences in
the presence of Father. He loved to tell her about the Father's dance.
They smiled as they discussed the great love they each experienced
in the presence of Father.

Adam shared with Eve every secret of his heart. As Father and
Adam had shared their lives together, so now Adam and Eve would
share their lives. The relationship between God and Adam would be
the model for the relationship between Adam and Eve. This was a
new stage in the ancient language—the free expressions of the heart
for other humans. Together the two of them shared one life, and
there was nothing to spoil their happiness.

The woman provided a brand new perspective for Adam's
world. Her insights and feelings opened up within him new realms
of spiritual reality. Through the sharing of their lives new words
were being added to the dictionary of the ancient language. Together they were discovering new realms of spiritual reality.

It was God's stated plan in the beginning that man and woman
should work together with a common purpose. As they lived together, Adam and Eve would enhance the ancient language with the
love they shared with each other. The home they built together
would be the beginning of the community of man.

God did not create a whole human race at one time. He started with just one man. This strategy is a key to understanding God's
approach to every human dilemma. He begins with a man. The stories related throughout the Scriptures testify to the consistency of
this divine strategy in the community of man.

The ancient language of Eden required a communal setting for its full development. Without a community the mother tongue would disappear. Language cannot exist apart from the culture formed by community. In the midst of community men and women shared the feelings of their hearts and the creative ideas formed in their thoughts. This mutual sharing of feelings, thoughts and ideas enhanced the vocabulary of the ancient language and empowered the community. Any attempt to restrict and repress this mutuality of life would destroy the original language of Eden. The ancient language of Eden thrives in a free and loving environment.

Naked and Not Ashamed

And the man and his wife were both naked and were not ashamed.   Genesis 2:25

In their nakedness Adam and Eve walked majestically through the garden and *in their weakness they were most invincible.* They were content to be the creatures living in the comforting care of their Creator. Pride of self was not yet born in the heart of man. Adam and Eve did not exult in themselves; they exalted in the Father who had created them. He was the love of their lives.

Their discussions during the daily excursions with Father were not peppered with the language of shame and guilt that would soon become a plague of twisted speech enveloping the earth. There was no notion of their nakedness and no sense of sin. Sin, shame and guilt were not found in the vocabulary of the ancient language spoken in Eden. In fact, no codes of morality dominated discussions in the garden. There was no sin and therefore no guilt or shame. Clothed in the presence of Father they experienced no shame.

Guilt is the emotional trauma created by what we have done, and shame is the result of the negative feelings about who we are. Because Adam and Eve walked in innocence before God there was no guilt, and because they were fully accepted by the Father's love there was no shame.

They lived in the weightlessness of grace and had not yet experienced the heaviness of shame. God accepted them wholly for who they were, and they could accept each other totally as they were. There was no gravitational pull downward into the dark realms of sin's shame because they lived in the buoyant atmosphere of God's amazing grace.

Eden's ancient language was a pure language not weakened by the slang of shame. Adam and Eve did not know rejection. Their lives were lived in the atmosphere of the full approval of Father's love. Walking in the favor of the Lord they flourished and matured. There were no opposite poles of light and darkness operating within them, muddling their spiritual speech.

Life was perfect in the garden, but dark clouds were appearing on the horizon. Adam and Eve were oblivious to the approaching darkness. The entrance of a new creature into the garden was about to wreck the love language of Eden.

Endnotes

1. *Spiritual Reformers*, Rufus Jones, p. 326.

2. *The Quotable Lewis*, Wayne Martindale and Jerry Root, Tyndale House Publishers, Wheaton, Illinois, 1989, p. 229.

3. *The Destiny of Man*, Nicolas Berdayaev, Harper Torch-books, New York, New York, 1960, p. 77.

4. *The Mind of the Maker*, Dorothy L. Sayers, Harper and Row, New York, New York, 1941, p. 61.

5. *Collected Poems*, T.S. Eliot, Harcourt Brace and Company, New York, 1962, p. 168.

Millenniums in a moment. A million miles in a step. An ocean in a drop. Volumes in a word. A race in a woman. A hell of suffering in an act. The depths of woe in a glance. The first chapter of Romans in Genesis three, six. Sharpest pain in softest touch. God mistrusted-distrusted. Satan embraced. Sin's door open. Eden's gate shut.[1]

S.D. Gordon

...that the choice of ways at any cross-road may be more important than we think; and that short cuts may lead to nasty places.[2]

C.S. Lewis

But one day man went away from God. And then he went farther away. He left home. He emigrated from God. And through going away he lost his mother tongue. Man left the native land of Eden and lost the art of speaking the native language of Eden. Through not hearing God speak He forgot the sounds of the heavenly language. His ears became dull. His perceptions blurred. He eventually lost the ability to speak heaven's native tongue.[3]

S.D. Gordon

CHAPTER 4

THE DEATH OF THE ANCIENT LANGUAGE

I fled Him, down the nights and down the days;
I fled Him, down the arches of the years;
I fled Him, down the labyrinthine ways
Of my own mind; and in the mist of tears

I hid from Him, and under running laughter.
Up vistaed hopes I sped;
And shot, precipitated,
Adown titanic glooms of chasmed fears,
From those strong Feet that followed, followed after.

But with unhurrying chase,
And unperturbed pace,
Deliberate speed, majestic instancy,
They beat—and a Voice beat
More instant than the Feet
"All things betray thee, who betrayest Me."[4]

Sadly, paradise never lasts forever. Man always finds a way to damage what love, freedom and inspiration have built. It seems as though every new discovery of man is ultimately transformed into an instrument of repression and ruin. In agreement with the law of the circular process, the simplicity and purity found in the beginning of all things ultimately deteriorates into the complexity and corruption in the ending of all things. Rolling the dice of personal choice too often sets off a series of catastrophes negatively affecting man's life and the lives of those around him. Tragically testifying to this truth are many of the technological discoveries of the last century. Even in his pursuit of the "good," man too often discovers new ways to create "evil."

Repeatedly, a recovered spiritual truth once bringing joy and freedom subtly and slowly gets swallowed up by religious *legalism*, rigid *formalism* and autocratic *rule*. This unholy triad is at the core of the religious code that corrupts every work of God. The delights of spiritual recovery are too frequently replaced by the heaviness of religious slavery—as spiritual principles degenerate into religious law.

To mankind's everlasting sorrow, the idyllic life in Eden was soon to be shattered by the entrance unto center stage of another life form emerging from the dark side of a created world. The serpent's knock at Eden's gate should have set off warning alarms reverberating throughout the garden. Answering the serpent's knock set into play events that would cause the serenity of this small, hallowed community in Eden to be lost for many ages.

The School of the Spirit

God's original plan had man as the ruler of earth. But the pathway to the place of co-regency was a predetermined road chosen by Father. Taking humanly devised bypasses down pitch-black alleyways of self-will would have the result of short-circuiting Father's purposes, plunging man into calamity.

Father's path precluded the preparation of man in the school of the Spirit and through the experiences of life. This spiritual education would ready him to effectively rule at the side of Father. But a scepter could not be put into his hand until the Word had been worked into his very nature and love reigned in his heart. Dressed in the regal robes of Father's nature and motivated by Father's love, he would be a ruler worthy of being called Father's son.

Though Adam had a good grasp of the words of Eden, he needed an experience with the Word. Knowledge can never be a substitute for experience. There could be no graduation until there was full maturation as a son.

Ongoing training in the ancient language of Eden was to be a significant part of his preparation. Mankind had to learn to harmonize his words with *the* Word. The words flowing from his lips had to synergize with the passion manifested in his actions in the affairs of men. Living in Father's presence was the natural environment for instruction in the ancient language. Father was hoping that man's skill in the mother tongue would mature into a rich language that would creatively express in vivid detail the spirit realm of Father.

It has taken me most of my adult life to learn these truths. My knowledge *of* the truth had puffed me up many sizes larger than my knowledge *in* the truth, creating a devastating illusion of spirituality. It is only in these last couple of years that I have come to understand that *true* knowledge arises out of *real* experiences with Father. My ancient language skills were almost nonexistent because I had chosen to pursue intellectual knowledge over spiritual learning. To my great regret, I see that I took a shortcut in the schools of man rather than pursuing the less traveled road of being schooled by the Spirit and the Word. Devoid of spiritual reality, I had chosen to walk in the spiritual knowledge of others, not realizing there can be no real secondhand life in God.

Adam and Eve were yet to learn this lesson. Bathed in a spring of earthly reality, they had not yet fully partaken of the wells of living water. Major gaps still existed in their experiences and knowledge of which they were unaware. These chambers of spiritual illiteracy and crevices of sacred ignorance were perilous inner caverns. Unless they maintained the presence of Father and were transformed into His likeness, they would be left vulnerable—exposed to the subtleties of the serpent's speech. This vulnerability could only be erased by an ongoing education in the presence of Father.

The Serpent Has a Question for Man

Detecting this spiritual handicap in man, satan was ready to make his move. He had patiently waited until the humans were secluded in a vulnerable place—when Father was not present with them. Following his cautiously calculated plan, satan in his serpent form proudly pranced into the garden preparing to inflict a mortal wound to the soul of God's beloved creature.

It seems clear that the woman never fully understood the portent of the two trees in the center of the garden, nor the nature of Father's restrictions. Was there a failure on Adam's part to communicate to Eve? Did he also fail to perceive the consequence-laden implications of Father's command not to eat from the tree of the knowledge of good and evil, thus minimizing the portent of that command? Eve's easy capitulation reveals her spiritual ignorance, immaturity and even subtle resentment of Father's restriction. Silently standing at her side, curiously Adam offered Eve no spiritual support in her ongoing dialog with the evil one.

Casting a dark cloud over God's word, the serpent questioned Eve. "Is that really what God said?" With one subtle question he rocked the world of man forever. The serpent assaulted the very heart of spirituality—man's trust in Father. Satan insinuated that man could not really trust God's word. With his treasonous question, he inserted himself between God and man. He would be the umpire, if you will, between God and man. As a counterfeit mediator he would grossly misrepresent Father. Throwing a blanket of ambiguity over the divine word, the father of all lies projected his own insidious nature onto the image of Father. The world of light, truth and open honesty in Eden was metamorphosing into a world of darkness, deceit, hidden agendas, illusions and lies.

> He subtly suggests that humankind's trust in God is ill-founded. Humankind cannot trust God for God will deceive them. In current jargon, it is a case of transference. The snake projects his own fork-tongued personality onto God and Adam and Eve choose to believe it.[5]
>
> John Shea

As the web was subtly being spun in the mind of Eve, her confidence was shaken. Mists of misunderstanding were rolling over her thinking processes creating a fog of insidious illusions. Struggling to pierce through this miasma to grasp the light of truth, her heart was beating faster and faster. Distorted desire was working its way down into her heart replacing the spiritual purity that once permeated her being. Blinded by chaotic confusion, her mind and her eyes were leading her ever closer to the precipice of a tragic choice. The fire of spiritual desire was sinking away, giving way to a new fire—the flame of lust. The cadence of lust's bewitching beat was overpowering her.

> *When the woman saw that the tree was good for food, and that it was a delight to the eyes, and that the tree was desirable to make one wise, she took from its fruit and ate.*
>
> Genesis 3:6

Suddenly all was quiet. The trap had been set, and the snare was awaiting the creature. On the part of the serpent this was neither sleight of hand, as exercised in a cunning card game, nor some magical trick, as seen in a traveling circus act. This was the master of illusion at his very best, weaving a delusion that cried out: "I must have that! I want it! I need it!"

In that fateful moment, Eve reached out to the tree, and in perfect step with the rhythm of evil's siren call, she took the fruit. In an exultation of daring, she bit greedily into it. Almost instantly the sweetness of the fruit turned bitter in her mouth. As that first bite was still sliding down her throat, the light in her soul already was slowly but steadily being extinguished. Eve doubled over in a spasm of unexpected agony. Spinning out of control, spiraling downward, she was rapidly floating further and further from her spiritual core; the gravitational pull of the Presence was rapidly losing its attracting power. She turned around and looked at the serpent—and the serpent smiled.

> ....and she gave also to her husband with her, and he ate.
>
> Genesis 3:6

Misery loves company. There is something innate in man that causes him to draw others into his own web of deceit. Without one seductive word from the lips of Eve, Adam accepted the fruit and joined in the complicity of Eve's criminal action without a backward glance. Both their eyes "were opened" as the serpent had promised. But they were opened to see things they were never meant to see.

Injection of the "Self" Virus

By eating of the tree of the knowledge of good and evil, by willing other than what God willed, man became unholy. Dying to the holy, heavenly image, he now lived in the awakened bestial image of the serpent. The animal being had swallowed up the celestial being, and Adam and Eve then had common flesh, brittle bones, bestial members, and needed bestial clothing.

> Man was now separated from God: Lusting after the earthly, the holy anointing oil, given of Christ, was dried up; he became shut up in a gross, bestial image, for his flesh now belonged to the earth and to death; the dominion of this world now dwelt within him.[6] Jacob Boehme

As the virus released by their actions permeated their beings, the light of the most holy place within the spirit of man grew dim.

In the inner man, the power of the soul gradually began to subordinate the rule of the spirit. Cataclysmic shifts in the nature of man were set in motion that would not be set right till the coming of the Second Adam.

In the beginning there was only one will—the will of Father—and all creation lived in harmony under this solitary rule. The rebellious action of man now introduced another will into the universe—the will of the flesh. As Adam's will supplanted Father's will, an eerie echo sounded throughout Father's created world. For the first time there was more than one will in the universe, and all nature began to groan. All creation immediately felt the impact of man's treason. Nature's silent sobbing sounds will not cease until man returns to the ancient garden and the many wills are once more merged into glorious union with the Father's will.

Critically wounded by the injection of the "self" virus, man became spiritually disabled. The focus of his life became inverted as he began to dwell on his needs and desires. The true direction of spiritual life was meant to be upward toward the heavenly atmosphere, but now man's life was turning inward and downward. As the memory of Father's presence began to slowly fade, man's spiritual energies irresistibly declined.

Scrambled in a maze of linguistic disorder, the spiritual speech patterns and heavenly grammar of the ancient language were disappearing. Sadly, the words of the old love language began to sink into a sea of forgetfulness. With a dulling of the ears and blurring of the spiritual perceptions, the language of Father was ultimately replaced by another language—the language of self.

The Birth of Moralism

Coupled with the emergence of this new and deadly language was the development of an evil and darkened consciousness. The serpent's promise became a reality, but not with the results the man and woman had hoped for. The shortcut down the dark back streets of self-will resulted in a new awareness of themselves. The result was immediately obvious. They had not become gods. In fact, they were being reshaped into a lower creation, their unique personalities damaged, and their consciousness coming under the domination of a new fleshly law.

A crippled consciousness would now be the rudder of man's darkened soul. For the first time, man knew good, and he knew evil.

This knowledge would inexorably replace the loving voice of Father. On that day morality was born. *Moralism became the substitute for spirituality.* Living in the presence of Father, man had been sustained by Father's breath. His life had been based upon the power of the Presence; now it would be based upon the enforcement of the law—the law of good and evil. He would now be defined by doing good and avoiding evil.

This new law would be the means of judging and evaluating oneself and others. Rather then seeing each other in the light of God's image, mankind would value and judge one another in the light of performance and conformity to the new fleshly law.

Man would forever experience the conflict between these two opposing laws—the law of the Spirit and the law of the flesh. The law of the Spirit would always be reminding him, though dimly, of the ancient language and the Presence of Father. The law of the flesh would insidiously obscure that memory as it enforced its own rules of procedure. These laws of behavior and procedure would become the basis of all future religions.

Seeking to enforce this homespun morality on others, all future cultures would emphasize the need for humanity to live by imposed rules from without rather than being motivated by the inward life of the Spirit. In some ways these outward laws would serve as a temporary protection for man until a new law could come—the law of grace and mercy resident in Jesus.

Religion became a partner in crime, seeking to control its members by moral legislation rather than helping, or at least releasing, them to find their own way back to the ancient garden and the empowering Presence. Presuming to be mouthpieces for the Father, religious leaders would arise to establish themselves as the authority in the community of God. Tradition and legalism would replace the life of the Spirit.

Father Has a Question for Adam

Meanwhile, back in the garden Adam and Eve stood rooted to the spot where they had thrown it all away, lost in the solitude of a frightening awareness of what they had done. Rewinding and replaying their actions again and again in their dazed minds, Adam and Eve trembled with fear of the consequences of their actions. Never had they felt such overwhelming terror. Retreating inwardly into their darkened deliberations, they experienced a deep sense of loneliness permeating their very souls. Meanwhile, a voice was attempting to break through the deep musings of their minds. Suddenly, they were arrested by the penetrating voice as it finally reached into the depths of their inner retreat. Rushing for the nearest tree, they attempted to hide from the voice.

"Adam, where art thou?"

"Who told you that you were naked?"

"Have you eaten from the tree
that I commanded you not to eat from?"

Questions are powerful tools to probe inward parts. The technique of psychological questioning is used in the psychiatrist's office as well as in the courtroom to find out the truth of a matter. Searching questions pierce the darkness of obfuscation, forcing man to confront the realities of his life. They compel us to examine our shame and our guilt, the destructive results of our wayward actions.

Father is the Master of the probing question, and as we will see in a later chapter, His Son also had the powerful gift of asking just the right question. It is of extreme importance that you understand the essential difference between the interrogations of man and the insightful searching questions of Father. Man's investigations are undertaken to expose and condemn. *Father's questions come to reveal and heal.*

Trembling at the sound of Father's voice, Adam and Eve attempted to hide themselves physically as well as psychologically. Hiding is man's perfected reaction to the horror of his actions and a natural response to the negative experiences of his life. Pulling the proverbial blanket over our heads gives us a sense of protection and security, albeit false. Through the years, man would refine this inward flight, creating great psychological impairment to his inner being. His only chance for healing is to remove the emotional coverings and in open honesty expose himself to the loving eyes of Father.

Regrettably, much of my life was spent on the pathway of this inward flight, as I sought to hide from the pain of what I perceived as my negative existence. Fearing to face the reality of my failures, I sought refuge in concealment. I lived under a false assumption that what others did not know would somehow protect me from increased pain and guilt. Fear of exposure hounded me, paralyzing much of my spiritual life. I did not understand that exposure was the only sure path to spiritual and emotional healing. Fear of exposure led me to the door of falsehood. When caught in a wrong action, I would simply lie to myself and others rather than expose myself.

To heal man, Father must expose man. Man's deep fear is that exposure will lead to even more emotional pain and condemnation. Man has good reason to fear unveiling himself. Self-disclosure more often than not leads to condemnation and judgment by others, even in the Church. But Father's questions are posed in order to enable us to see what He already knows. His questions help us arrive at a safe place of self-realization, where forgiveness and grace can do their mysterious and majestic work.

Hiding and Blaming—
Man's Answers to Father's Questions

The man said, "The woman whom You gave to be with me, she gave me from the tree, and I ate."
...The woman said, "The serpent deceived me, and I ate."
Genesis 3:12-13

The couple had now lost all control of the situation. They could not get a grip on reality and moved blindly, it seems, from one sin to another. A chain reaction of deception and denial that had been set in motion was establishing future patterns of behavior for man. Rather than deal with his sin, man now introduced two very powerful psychological tools for attempting to avoid the consequences of his failures in life—*hiding and blaming.*

In hiding and blaming, man fashioned a whole new vocabulary, as it were, to replace the spiritual vernacular of honesty and openness that characterized the ancient language of Eden. This dark form of communication was developed in an effort to protect man from facing the consequences of the horrible realities of his life. Thus began the dialect of blame shifting, rationalization, deception, lies, coded language, irresponsibility and shame-speech.

And Eve originated what would become the classic copout: "The devil made me do it." Enter the world of recrimination, injustice, scapegoating, and irresponsibility."[7]

John Shea

The old mother tongue began to disappear as self-talk took greater control of man's speech patterns. Self-love, self-defense and self-advancement were becoming the rule of the interior life of man. The image of self was replacing the image of God.

Now let us weep together as we examine the deterioration of the ancient language of Eden and the developing dialects of the language of self.

Language of Doubt

Now the serpent was more crafty than any beast of the field which the Lord God made. And he said to the woman, "Indeed, has God said, 'You shall not eat from any tree of the garden'?"   Genesis 3:1

The matrix of the garden was an environment of total, loving trust and obedience to the spoken words of God. Love and trust were the root grammatical structures of the mother tongue. They constituted the framework of man's outer environment as well as the structure for his inner world. All things were held together by Father's word—the outer world and man's inner space.

Having carefully followed this developing structure, the evil one knew the only way to break it down was to create a fracture in man's trust in the words of God. With subtlety, he carefully planted a seed of doubt in the thought processes of the woman. Man and woman were only accustomed to honesty and open communication, never having experienced any other language in Father's company. But then the evil one introduced a new form of speech—deception and insinuation.

The cunning of satan opens a mortal chasm in the soul of man. As the woman pondered the serpent's words, a hint of doubt began to take shape—doubt that would eventually grow into an act of betrayal and a breakdown in man's trust in Father.

Trust, so essential to the language of Eden, was shattered in that moment. That one small entertainment of doubt would eventually mushroom into a whole system of unbelief. The new language of that system would express this doubt in myriad streams of human thought—skepticism, cynicism, atheism and humanism. Man began to not only doubt Father's words, but also to question His love, misinterpret His actions and even move to the point of questioning His very existence.

Language of Pride

"For God knows that in the day you eat from it your eyes will be opened, and you will be like God, knowing good and evil."   Genesis 3:5

In his plan to bring down God's beloved creature, the serpent proceeded to his next strategy—the appeal to pride. Man had lived contentedly in the humble place of the creature, understanding that all he was and all he had were a result of Father's loving power. Man was the creature, and Father was the Creator. Seeking to disrupt that order, the serpent stroked man's pride. "You will be like God." Man pondered this. Could it be possible? Could man also be a god? The beguiling door to divine possibilities cracked upon satan's sly words, and the man and woman took the bait and slipped through the entryway.

Where his speech once was filled with praise and worship directed toward God, man's language degenerated into the slutty speech of pride-filled talk—pride of accomplishments, pride of knowledge, pride of strength and pride of life. The humble language of man was being twisted into a focus upon who he was and what he could do. Love of self would now dominate his communications with others. Self-preoccupation quickly grew to overwhelm man's speech habits, robbing him of the ability and even desire to intimately relate to Father and effectively communicate with others in the ancient tongue.

Language of Twisted Desire

When the woman saw that the tree was good for food, and that it was a delight to the eyes, and that the tree was desirable to make one wise, she took from its fruit and ate; and she gave also to her husband with her, and he ate.
                                    Genesis 3:6

In his desire to disrupt the flow of spiritual delight and desire between Creator and creature, the serpent again shifted the focus of desire away from Father's will to man's needs and wants. Eyes that were once filled with the light found in Father's presence were being clouded over with a perverted form of desire—lust. The old words of worship and praise were being substituted with murmurs of selfish pleasure. The desire for momentary gratification was overwhelming the once content and grateful heart.

A floodgate of all sorts of evil desires rushed through the door opened by the woman—inordinate desires for money, power, sex, and possessions would eat away at all spiritual desire. Rather than becoming gods as hinted at by the serpent, they unwittingly became slaves—slaves to their own corrupted cravings. Rather than ruling over desire, desire would rule over them. The language of man evolved further, filled with all manner of lustful talk eroding even further the pure speech of the love talk of Eden.

Language of Shame

He said, "I heard the sound of You in the garden, and I was afraid because I was naked; so I hid myself."

Genesis 3:10

Adam had never experienced fear. Totally secure in his belovedness, he confidently performed his work in the garden paradise. Invigorated by the freedom he experienced in the presence of Father, Adam joyfully worked on Father's behalf tending the garden. Clothed with a sense of divine worth, he was never troubled with thoughts of insignificance or failure. Love of Father motivated him, not duty or addictions.

The serpent's goal to divide Adam and Father and to destroy the peace in this ancient place was beginning to be realized. When his seductive work was done, the serpent needed only to step back and let the chips fall where they may.

In a blinding, horrific realization of what they had done, Adam and Eve recoiled in shame. Falling to the ground, they groaned deep within their spirits at their treasonous deed. A penetrating sensation of shame was stripping away the clothing of personal worth they had worn in the presence of Father. Father! Oh no! They became paralyzed at the thought of Father. For the very first time ever, they feared the presence of Father. What would He think? What would He do? "We have failed Him!" The pain was almost unbearable.

A pervasive sense of shame is the ongoing premise that one is fundamentally bad, inadequate, defective, unworthy, or not fully valid as a human being.[8]

                                                    Lewis B. Smedes

Thus, destructive thoughts of shame were introduced into the being and language of man. At first subtle, eventually they would saturate his psyche to be acted out in his daily life. Shame would drive mankind in the wrong direction—away from the presence of Father. This is the destructive power of shame. Rather than draw us to the place of healing it drives us to run and hide from God and others. Unable to bear the guilt of our actions we hunt for places of seclusion that result in a numbing sense of loneliness. Enter the language of self-hate, compulsive comparison with others, unworthiness, and voraciously needing the approval of others.

I know a lot about shame. Much of my life was lived in the house of shame. At first, it was subtle and mostly unconscious, but I could feel shame's debilitating presence encroaching on my inner thoughts. I could not have explained exactly what it was; I just knew that there was something very wrong with me. Life went on, and the accumulation of years of failure sharply defined the shame. It began drifting to the surface of my mind more and more.

I felt the awful weight of shame for my failures as a son, as a husband, as a father and finally, as a preacher. Shame depreciated my every attempt to please Father. Years of a steady infusion of shame finally left me spiritually disabled in my mid-life years. Only when I discovered the loving Presence of Father, or rather, when He found me, did the shame lift from off me.

Man helplessly wallows in the mire of guilt and shame until the coming of Jesus. In Jesus the filthy clothing of shame is replaced with the clothing of the Spirit.

The pain that Adam and Eve felt did not begin to compare to the pain of loss pulsating in Father's heart. Though deeply hurt, He could not leave His children to wander the world uncovered. He already had a plan in the works that would take care of everything, but until its appointed time, Father would provide a covering for His still beloved children.

Language of Rejection

*Therefore the Lord God sent him out from the garden of
Eden...*   Genesis 3:23

Man had only known the Presence of Father. He had never
lived a day of his life without the comforting sense of God all
around him. His eyes first opened beholding the face of God radiant with love, and he had known only the security of living in that
all-encompassing love. Now he was banished from the place of the
Presence. There would be no more daily walks filled with sweet
nothings being spoken in his ear. As the human retreated further
into his own dark self-absorbed world, he became deeply aware of a
bone-chilling feeling of isolation. While relationship with Father is
not totally destroyed, it is distorted and detached.

This detachment is the source of the profound sense of loneliness. At the numbing center of this loneliness man experiences a
deep ache and longing for what could have been. This alienation and
loneliness is woven into the very warp of modern man. His guilt and
shame have driven him inward into a psychological alienation and
spiritual loneliness. In this hermetically sealed condition he is prey
to all the ongoing lies of worthlessness and shame.

C.S. Lewis said it well when he said he felt like a man brought
out under naked heaven, on the edge of a precipice, into the teeth of
a wind that came howling from the Pole.

The communal memory of what was lost in that ancient garden
creates a psychic ache in the soul of man. Though unaware of its origin, he nevertheless seeks to fill this vacuum of loneliness and rejection with any and every sort of activity and relationship, or else he
retreats into seclusion. The language of man is rife with expressions
of names for this deep sense of loneliness and spiritual rejection.

What man does not understand is, he was driven out so that he
might be brought back, changed by the realization that Father had always pursued him. The tree of life was kept *from him* for a time that
it might be kept *for him* for an eternity. In the book of Genesis, we see
man driven out of Paradise and away from the Tree of Life. In the
Book of Revelation, we see the gate to Eden reopened and man once
again brought into the garden with a special invitation to come eat
from the Tree of Life. The Son of man will be the one to swing open
that ancient gate and help man reclaim the precious ancient language.

Endnotes

1. *Quiet Talks About Jesus*, S.D. Gordon, Destiny Image Publishers, Shippensburg, Pennsylvania, 2003, pp. 21-22.

2. *The Quotable Lewis*, Wayne Martindale and Jerry Root, p. 231.

3. *Quiet Talks About Jesus*, S.D. Gordon, p. 11.

4. *The Hound of Heaven*, Thompson, www.geocities.com/Athens/Troy/1787/thompson.html.

5. *The Challenge of Jesus*, John Shea, Thomas Moore Press, Chicago, Illinois, 1975, p. 115.

6. *The Lost Passions of Jesus*, Don Milam, Destiny Image Publishers, Shippensburg, Pennsylvania, 1998, p. 23.

7. *The Challenge of Jesus*, John Shea, p. 117.

8. *Shame and Grace*, Lewis B. Smedes, Harper Collins, New York, New York, 1993, p. 3.

Then, came, at a predetermined moment, a moment in time and of time,
A moment not out of time, but in time, in what we call history: transecting, bisecting the world of time, a moment in time but not like a moment of time,
A moment in time, but time was made through that moment: for without the meaning there is no time, and that moment of time gave the meaning.[1]

T.S. Eliot

Everything in Christ astonishes me. His spirit overawes me, and His will confounds me. Between Him and whoever else in the world, there is no possible term of comparison. He is truly a being by Himself. I search in vain in history to find the similar to Jesus Christ, or anything which can approach the gospel. Neither in history, nor humanity, not the ages, nor nature, offer me anything with which I am able to compare it or explain. Here everything is extraordinary.[2]

Napoleon

CHAPTER 5

JESUS—GOD'S LAST WORD TO MAN

The entrance of sin uninvited into the human community disrupted Father's plan and broke His heart. Lonely and lost, man left the ancient garden to take up residence in a world of shame, guilt and isolation. Outside the gate of Eden, a new community took shape—a home where the freedom and love once known in the primitive garden became a melancholic memory. Only a few relics remaining in man's world reminded him of his previous life.

The patriarchs and prophets were among the few who attempted to recover remnants of that ancient life. Their lives and words prophetically testified to the spiritual discoveries they made that transcended their times. On tiptoe they peeked into the spirit realm faintly catching a glimpse of the Coming One.

Having lost his mother tongue, man developed a new language reflective of his new life. The result was a dialect devoid of the passionate words of the language spoken in Eden. Even though man had wandered far away from Father and had lost his ability to speak the ancient language, deep within his empty soul there was still an irresistible longing for all he had once been. Restless and wandering, he was hopelessly homesick.

Where once man lived in the presence of Father, he has grown accustomed to life without Father. He is more aware of the *absence* of God than the *presence* of God. The history of man from that ancient garden to our present day is a story of heartbreaking flight from the Presence. Haunted by shame and guilt, he is tortured by his own inward darkness, no longer able to feel the love of Father. The tragedies of war, the ravages of disease, natural calamities, economic poverty, and seemingly unanswered prayers have all served to obscure Father's love. Merely talking about the love of God and the God of love is easy, although human beings trapped in life's cruel realities feel God's cold-hearted silence rather than God's love.[3]

Ancient memories from time to time surface, arousing a holy desire to see the Face once more. At the same time, religion tells him to fear the face of Presence, driving him ever deeper into hiding in a morass of lonely despair and shameful disgrace. He fears he can never be accepted into Father's presence. Carrying so much sin and failure, he is desperately running out of spiritual fuel in his journey away from Eden. Flight and pursuit, shame and acceptance, these are the tensions within man causing restlessness and frantic searching for meaning and love.

The entrance of sin, while disrupting Father's plan, in no way defeated it. God was forever committed to the beings He had created. His love would prevail. There was never a question about that! He let it be known to the principalities and powers that He Himself would, at a predetermined time, intervene and rescue man from the devastation unleashed by the evil one on Father's precious planet. God would not—could not—in disappointment and anger wipe the thought of man from the slate of His memory. His heart still throbbed with recollections of the wonderful times He had enjoyed with Adam.

In order to hold in trust the ancient ways and bring forth the divine plans, Father chose a race of people through whom He could prepare the way for the second Adam. In this *interim* time the law was given to protect man until grace could come. It was also to remind man of his own inability to work the plan through his own efforts. The sweat of religion has never produced anything of lasting worth. The demands of the law were meant to expose his moral frailty, not to be a goal for his religious life. Unfortunately, man's attempts to keep the law thwarted the very purpose of the law and became a heavy burden promoting further remorse and humiliation.

Behind the *shadow* of the law and the tabernacle lay a hidden reality, waiting to be exposed in the proper time. Like coded messages meant to be unlocked, they prophetically spoke of One to come who would free them from the need for religious performance—a routine that could never remove the crippling sense of shame and guilt. Fortunately, during those dark days there were those who were able to catch a glimpse beyond the prophetic symbolism and catch a view of the coming time when grace will reign. These prophetic peeks drove these seers to transcend the reality of their times.

At the right time, Father moved out from behind the shroud of mystery obscuring His presence among men. *For God so loved the world...* The love that created the world would save the world. Wrapped in a bit of human tapestry, Jesus would come as Father's love gift to man. The mystery of it all was that He was always coming. Before mankind cried out, help was *already* on the way.

"From the eternal warmth of the 'communion of glory' with His Father, the Son of Man descended into the cold abyss of human misery." [4] Undressing in His earthly descent, Jesus stepped into the human race as one of our own. Exiting through the bright light of Heaven's gate—an exit witnessed by the consternation of hosts of angels—He crossed the threshold into the misery and hopelessness enclosing the existence of humankind.

> ...The Word who makes the world is identical to the Word who saves the world... He brings his Divinity down into the misery of our humanity, and he lifts that very misery up into himself. He who is the key to the city dies outside the city. [5]
>
> Robert Farrar Capon

Who is Jesus?

And they said to her, "Woman, why are you weeping?"
She said to them, "Because they have taken away my
Lord, and I do not know where they have laid Him."
When she had said this, she turned around, and saw Jesus
standing there, and did not know that it was Jesus.

John 20:13-14

Before we explore the work and words of Jesus, we must understand the person of Jesus. One of the problems of modern Christianity is that we are more consumed with explanations of Christ than we are in experiences with Christ. Through the use of our spiritual jargon and theological explanations, we have succeeded in weaving a web of confusion that almost completely obscures the reality of Jesus.

While working on a publishing project with Tommy Tenney and his father, I had scheduled a conference call to discuss some issues related to the project. In the middle of our conversation, Tommy's father turned the conversation to a more personal nature. I'll never forget these loving words he directed to his son. "Tommy, before Jesus was a principle, He was a person."

This is the crux of our dilemma in these days. The church has been more concerned with the principles of Christianity than the heart of Christianity—the person of Jesus. We have elevated the study of Christ over the pursuit of Christ. Intellectual knowledge has displaced spiritual pursuit. One dreadful result of this intellectual approach is the judgments we make of one another based upon our theological persuasions. *We have made Jesus into a doctrine we must believe rather than a person we love.* Then, we judge and condemn one another on the basis of those doctrinal persuasions rather than the reality of our personal experiences with Christ. *How sad Father must be!*

As the first century faded into the sunrise of the second century, men wandered from the vitality of the primitive church's intimate experience with Christ. In an effort to defend the essence of who Jesus is, systematic theology was born. The Church became obsessed with *explaining Him* rather than *experiencing Him.* Each succeeding generation has, in its own way, added to the theological definition of who He is. We have carved out our religious creeds, and these fragile carvings have become the core of our belief system, assuring us that we are worshiping the right Jesus. Or are we? Is it possible we have made an idol out of our theology?

From the second century forward, theologians wrestled with the divine and human natures of Jesus, eventually settling on a creedal agreement on his hypostatic (human and divine) nature. They battled over the nature of His essence, creating fissures in the Body of Christ as theology split off into various forms of gnostic and patristic positions.

Medieval times denuded and stripped Him of His authentic self, transforming Him into some sort of mystical apparition. Each succeeding generation added its own humanistic descriptions gradually morphing Jesus into a theological construct. In our times, men have forced Him into all manner of theological straightjackets to strengthen their own religious stances.

Separated now by two centuries of theological development, the Church, by and large, has lost the awe-inspiring reality of Jesus. Blaise Pascal made a powerful indictment on the Christianity of his day that is an appropriate analogy of our own times: God created man in His image, and man returned the favor!

We are guilty of reshaping Christ into the image of our own personal beliefs. We have made Him small so we can fit Him into our pathetically circumscribed spirits. Preserving our personal theologies has been more important than the pursuit of true ultimate reality. Our knowledge of Christ has been forged through the study of books and sermons from the pulpit, rather than through the personal experiences of life and revelations of the Spirit.

Sadly, religion has taken away our Lord, and we do not know where it has laid Him. He has been misplaced in a labyrinth of religious rhetoric. This is the challenge of our times—the recovery of Christ. We will not discover Him in the study halls of religion, but in the secret places of the Spirit.

We are not seeking to understand His genetic code as theology endeavors to do in the study of the nature of the God-man. We are not looking for His chemical makeup or blood type. We are not in quest of new theological language so that we can better explain who He is. We are not interested in Christology; we are interested in Christ! We are desperate to rediscover the reality of who He is and experience the wonder of His life.

As Robert Farrar Capon says, He is the Divine Suspect who is behind every meaningful thing in the universe, and we seek that reality. Through the centuries there have always been those who were able to break free from the matrix of the ghastly imagery created by systematic theology and grotesque illusions imposed by her priests and preachers. They are part of a hidden remnant that can be traced back to the ancient times.

These mystics and reformers have passionately explored the realms of spiritual reality in their quest of Jesus. They longed to connect with Heaven's reality. The syntax of the ancient language could be recognized in the grandeur of their words. This spiritual remnant, most often persecuted by the religious order of their day, were not to be denied the Christ they pursued. The magnetism of His presence relentlessly drew them on in their often lonely pursuit of Jesus.

I have read many of their writings and have been overwhelmed by the spiritual reality evident in their words, exposing the shallowness of our times. They were luminaries in the dark days of the Church and provide us with a most important link to the spiritual heritage we have lost. Most of us are aware of the heroes of the Reformation—Martin Luther, John Calvin, Ulrich Zwingli and others. But did you know that there was a parallel stream flowing throughout those same days? It was a stream that church history has by and large ignored.

Traveling this spiritual tributary, were men most of us have never heard of. Men of whom the world (the Church?) was not worthy—Platonist Peter Sterry, Anabaptist Hans Denck, Johann Bunderlin, poet Thomas Traherne, Sebastian Franck, Sebastian Castellio, and others. These men were deeply concerned about the direction the Reformation was taking. Many of the reformers were allowing passion for theological truth to override the pursuit of Christ. The reformation wars had become very ugly. First they fought the Catholic Church, who they saw as the spawn of satan, then they turned on each other. I don't know about you, but I don't want to be known by the label "fightin' fundy." This same spirit of spiritual assassination is still prevalent in our times. While we can't burn the "heretic" at the stake, we *can* castigate him from the pulpit and our television programs. *And, by God, we will!*

This lonely band of "outsiders" stood resolutely against that tide of division and hatred. Though the reformers rejected and persecuted them cruelly, they remained undaunted in their passion for Christ. They had, by God's grace, been lifted out of the mainstream of mediocrity and placed upon the lonely path of chasing their dream—the belief that it is possible to know God and to live in His courts. These were reckless men—desperate, no matter the cost, to rediscover the reality of Christ. Their words cry out to us today.

> The Fullness of the juncture of God and man is seen only in Christ. In Him, "God and man are one, one Love, one Life, one Likeness. He is the Pattern, the unspoiled Image, the Eternal Word, and He is too the Head of our race. In Him the Divine Spirit and the human spirit 'are twined into one.' If you want to see God, then see Christ. If you want to see what the Seed in us can blossom into when it is unhampered by sin, again see Christ. He is the

Life-giving Spirit who can penetrate other spirits, who
broods over the soul as the creative Spirit brooded over
the waters, and who, when received, makes us radiant
with Love, which is the only truth of religion.[6]

Peter Sterry

It is Christ who first reveals the full measure of love, who
makes us see the one adequate Object of love, and who
forges within our human spirits the invisible bonds of a
love that binds us forever to Him who so loved us.[7]

Thomas Traherne

We find in that divine Face, that infinitely deep and lu-
minous Personality who spoke as no man ever spake, who
loved as none other ever loved, who saw more in humanity than anybody else has ever seen, and who felt as no
other person ever has that He was one in heart and mind
and will with God.[8]   Rufus M. Jones

Christ has been called the Image, the Character, the Expression of God, yes, the Glory and Effulgence of His
Splendour, the very Impression of His Substance, so that
in Him God Himself whom we see and hear and perceive
in Christ. In Him God becomes visible and His nature is
revealed. Everything God is, or know, or wills, or possesses, or can do, is incarnated in Christ and put before
our eyes. Everything that can be said of God can as truly
be said of Christ.[9]   Sebastian Castellio

Jesus Comes to Reveal the Father

Man was born looking into Father's eyes. After being driven
from the garden, man attempted to retain the image of Father's face
in his consciousness. But over time the memories inexorably
slipped away into the dim recesses of his subconscious. Trying as
best he could, man could no longer remember Father's face. In an
effort to somehow redeem the fading image, men constructed idols.
These idols served as human symbols of the Father they had lost. To
his great harm, man replaced the worship of Father with the worship
of images. This prompted Father's restrictions in the law against the

worship of idols. He knew the disastrous effect they would have on man's soul.

We don't construct heathen idols in our days, you might think, but the Church has been guilty of worshiping false idols instead of engaging in true worship. Religion has constructed false images of the Father, misrepresenting His nature and falsifying His work among His people. Angry religious leaders replaced the smiling face of a loving Father with the threatening image of a Creator barely restraining Himself from wiping out His rebellious creation. Outstretched arms were turned into a shaking finger. This deeply grieves Father, who still stands on the porch, with the light on, watching intently for the return of His beloved son.

> *No one has seen God at any time; the only begotten God*
> *who is in the bosom of the Father, He has explained Him.*
>   John 1:18

From that place of intimacy, in the bosom of the Father, Jesus came to *exegete*, or to give explanation of Father's real nature. The most accurate, compassionate theology is the one that emerges from the place of passion, from the side of the Father. From that place of intimacy and union Jesus brings a precise, passionate, compelling, and liberating revelation of the living God. From His place at the edge of eternity Jesus delivered mystifying, profound, never before heard declarations of the heavenly truth.

His information about Father did not come from intense study of the Torah but from His life in the presence of Father. The images He constructed of Father were in direct contrast to the vengeful God that dominated the teachings of Israel's religious leaders. Unlike the theology of today, Jesus words came from His intimacy with His loving Father, not from studies in a seminary. The depth and reality of his words came from leaning on Father's breast, not from filling His mind with men's interpretations of Father.

> Jesus is God coming down to woo man up to Himself again. "Jesus was God letting man see the beauty of His face and listen to the music of His voice, and feel the irresistibly gentle drawing of His presence." He had wrapped Himself up in a bit of human tapestry so He

could move among men without blinding their eyes. Now
He looks through the strands.[10]   S.D. Gordon

Father has always been speaking, but mankind has not always
been able to perceive Father's words. Religion and self-love perverted man's powers of perception. The light in his spirit had been
darkened by his focus on self. Father had sent many in His name declaring the certainties of the heavenly realm. He had chosen many
forms of speech to reveal Himself to men, but now as the writer of
Hebrews said, He comes speaking through His Son. This is Father's
final and greatest Word.

> We must think of the Son always, so to speak, streaming
> forth from the Father, like light from a lamp, or heat from
> a fire, or thoughts from a mind. He is the self-expression
> of the Father—what the Father has to say. And there never
> was a time when He was not saying it.[11]   C.S. Lewis

Jesus came to reveal the invisible God and unlock the mystery
of His Being. Descriptions and details of Father undoubtedly are
most likely to be accurate when delivered by One who has lived in
His Presence and is of His nature. The Son presented the Father in
loving, intimate detail, determined to expose the lies that had grown
up around the mystery. Father's glory would be concealed no longer,
for it walked onto the human stage in the form of a living, breathing representation of the almighty One.

> Jesus shares with us the darkness of what it is to be with-
> out God as well as showing forth the glory of what it is to
> be with God.[12]   Frederich Buechner

Jesus compassionately, but relentlessly, worked to remove the
veil concealing Father's face. Religion had it hung to protect itself
from being revealed as empty and powerless. Driving Him was an
intense yearning that others might know Father as He knows Him.
He knew Father wasn't angry with His creation, but was yearning
for His sons and daughters to return! From the very beginning of
His time of ministry here on earth, Jesus tirelessly taught this truth.
God was not a vengeful, angry Being from whom they had to hide.
Speaking a language from another place, Jesus opened vistas to
them they had only dimly seen in dreams while sleeping in their

beds. The very depths of their beings were profoundly stirred as they drank in every word of Jesus.

> *"Look at the birds of the air, that they do not sow, nor reap nor gather into barns, and yet your heavenly Father feeds them.* **Are you not worth much more than they?** *...But if God so clothes the grass of the field, which is alive today and tomorrow is thrown into the furnace,* **will He not much more clothe you?** *You of little faith!*
>
> Matthew 6:26,30 (emphasis added)

Mesmerized by the conviction and authority of the words Jesus used when talking of Father, the people of Israel followed Him everywhere He went. They were afraid to lose sight of Him. He could not avoid the crowds. They were, of course, desperate for the miracles He seemed to easily perform, but their hungry souls cried out to experience the reality of the truth he was declaring. The attractive portrait he was painting of a heavenly Father was gradually erasing the grotesque, fearful image of God religion had imposed on them. Man hungered once more for the Presence.

The Jews' fascination with the miraculous works of Jesus blinded them to the real miracle! They seemed oblivious to the divine Presence that dwelt within this extraordinary man. The Glory was with them, but they were unable to detect its presence. The Glory is powerful, majestic, and overwhelming; yet it is enigmatic, veiled, and mysterious. The enigma of the Glory was lifted in the person of Jesus.

Throughout His ministry Jesus consistently used the word *Father* when communicating to His listeners. In the Gospel of John, the word "Father" is recorded more than 90 times. Jesus' mission on earth was to reconcile mankind to Father God. The title "Father" superceded all their revelations of Jehovah; Jesus gave it preeminence over every other name for God. Jesus' introduction of the name "Father" created a tidal wave of totally new understanding of the Lord God, and it inspired men to seek Him with new fervor. Jesus was replacing fear with faith—faith that Father loved them and that they were not abandoned.

It is important for us to understand that Jesus was not just looking for a word that would help man interpret God. He was not offering an anthropological model to explain the unexplainable

Almighty. The word Father, in its most sublime and noble sense, is the essence of who God is. It is intrinsic to His nature and unique to His relationship with the creation. Out of His Father heart, mankind was birthed. Father was, is, and always shall be Initiator, Creator, Protector, Lover, Provider, Sustainer, and the Beginning and End of all things.

> Nay, the fatherhood which Scripture predicates of God is not something which God is like, but something which He essentially is. The really startling fact is this, that instead of the living fatherhood being a reflection of human fatherhood, it is human fatherhood which is an intended reflection of the divine![13]

The Parable of the Loving Father

The most famous of Jesus' stories compellingly and compassionately illustrates in a most dramatic way the loving heart of Father God. The story is traditionally called the parable of the prodigal son. This parable could be more appropriately called the parable of the loving Father. He is the key figure in the story. The story centers around His unending, fathomless love for all His sons.

The story of Adam might have been Jesus' inspiration for this tender story. Just as Adam chose to abandon his Father in the ancient garden, so the prodigal leaves his father's home. Possibly driving him was a desire to prove himself. But, in actuality, he had nothing to prove to his father. He already had his complete love and approval. But a deep-seated need for approval lies deep within every man and woman, and it often drives us to desperate extremes. While usually derived from a lack of some sort in our material lives, it finds its deeper source in Adam's need to "win back" Father's approval. But the ironic truth is: He already had what he so desperately sought.

The prodigal's desire to find approval took him away from the *one* place where it could be found. His father's love allowed the prodigal the freedom to search in far places. Leaving home, the son found that the farther he got away from the voice of Father's unconditional love, the stronger was the pull to a "distant country." His journey, as the story goes, eventually left him lost, lonely, and loveless and digging for food in a pig sty.

Father has placed within each one of us an internal photo album that is a faithful reminder of a better place. I believe this is the *original* homesickness and is a fundamental part of the human nature. Our collective memory tells us that our true home is in the presence of Father, and He has left the light on waiting for our return.

> ...the ongoing yearning of the human spirit, the yearning for a final return, an unambiguous sense of safety, a lasting home. But beneath or beyond all that, "coming home" meant, for me, walking step by step toward the One who awaits me with open arms and wants to hold me in an eternal embrace.[14]   Henri Nouwen

In the midst of his despair and loneliness, the prodigal remembers. Ah yes, the marvelous power of a loving memory! There is Father who gave him everything he asked for and, though weeping, wished him well on his journey. Remembering Father and home decided it for him; he was going back. It may never be the same, but at least he would be home.

Author Henri Nouwen describes this desire as a self-serving repentance that offers the possibility of survival. In his efforts to prove himself, he had destroyed his life and brought much shame to the family name. Fortunately, his passion to return was more powerful than the shame that covered him.

The closer the son got to home, the clearer his memories became. He could seem to see Father's face more clearly with each step he took, and anticipation was growing. As he crested the hill upon which his home sat, he saw a figure get up from a rocker. It seemed to be peering intently in his direction. Suddenly, it took off running toward him. Father!

What he didn't know was that Father had been waiting every day since he had gone. Sitting on the front porch day after day, gazing longingly into the distance for his lost boy to return. As his father reached him and pulled him into a bear hug, the son started to give the speech he had so carefully prepared. "I'm not worthy... Make me as one of your servants." But his mouth was crushed into Father's shoulder, and he heard his father cry: "My son, my son, you've come home. You've come home!" No apologies requested. No recriminations given. No tough love conditions laid on the wayward son. Just, "Let's have a party!"

The scene then shifts to an encounter between the father and his eldest son. This son had no patience with or compassion for his younger brother. He was a screw-up. He and demanded and then wasted his inheritance and had dishonored the family. He needed to pay for his actions. Watching his father's exhibition of joy over his brother's homecoming infuriated the elder son. Was his father out of his mind? How could he just take that little traitor back without re-quiring one single thing from him? This was crazy! After all, he was the one who had worked hard his whole life on his father's behalf. He had never sinned against the family name. He had always been a good son, always faithfully working for his father.

In his account of the older brother in his book *The Return of the Prodigal Son*, Nouwen said: "There is so much frozen anger among the people who are so concerned about avoiding 'sin.' "[15] There are too many "older brothers" in the Body of Christ with judgmentalism, anger, and jealousy. Father's love must change their hearts too. So, Father sent His own unique Son into the world to demonstrate His love for all His sons. Jesus made a point of telling us over and over again, that if we see Him, we see Father. And He only did what Father does.

Endnotes

1. *The Collected Poems of T.S. Eliot*, T.S. Eliot, Harcourt Brace and Company, New York, 1962, "The Rock," p. 163.

2. *The Jesus I Never Knew,* Philip Yancey, Zondervan Publishers, Grand Rapids, Michigan, 1995, p. 83.

3. *A Life of Jesus*, Shusaku Endo, Paulist Press, New Jersey, 1973, p. 44.

4. *The Lost Passions of Jesus*, Don Milam, Destiny Image Publishers, Shippensburg, Pennsylvania, 1998, p. 120.

5. *The Fingerprints of God*, Robert Farrar Capon, Eerdmans, Grand Rapids, Michigan, 2000, pp. 11-12, 15.

6. *Spiritual Reformers in the 16th and 17th Century*, Rufus M. Jones, Beacon Hill, Boston, Massachusetts, 1914, p. 284.

7. *Spiritual Reformers*, Rufus M. Jones, pp. 332-333.

8. *Spiritual Reformers*, Rufus M. Jones, p. xlvi.

9. *Spiritual Reformers*, Rufus M. Jones, p. 61.

10. *Quiet Talks About Jesus*, S.D. Gordon, A.C. Armstrong & Son, 1906, p. 127.

11. *The Quotable Lewis*, Wayne Martindale and Jerry Root, Tyndale House Publishers, Wheaton, Illinois, 1989, p. 340.

12. *Telling the Truth*, Frederich Buechner, Harper San Francisco, San Francisco, California, 1977, p. 42.

13. *The Lost Passions of Jesus*, Don Milam, p. 96.

14. *The Return of the Prodigal Son*, Henri Nouwen, Doubleday, New York, New York, 1992, p. 6.

15. *The Return of the Prodigal Son*, Henri Nouwen, p. 71.

The form of the teaching of Jesus, the way in which he clothes his interior life in words, indubitably possesses an artistic character. The wealth of the style is remarkable. Jesus could tell a story in a very living, simple and arresting way; he knew how to stir the minds of the hearers with vigour; if necessary he could pour forth scorn with unmistakable energy, he could console with gentleness, humiliate with biting sarcasm, blame with bitterness, be indignant with intense vigour, and rejoice intensely. Everywhere he manifests his creative originality. Everything is brief, every word hits the target, all is concrete. There is never a word too much. His words always give the impression that they are self-evident. They seem as though they could never be any different from what they are, and this proves that they have issued from within in a living and spontaneous manner.[1]

Weidel

CHAPTER 6

RESTORING THE
ANCIENT LANGUAGE

In the archives of church tradition lies a little known story. After John the beloved disciple was released from prison on the island of Patmos, he returned to the city of Ephesus. The church founded by the ministry of the apostle Paul lovingly and joyfully received the venerated apostle of love into their midst. Gathering around the aging apostle, they listened for hours to his awe-inspiring personal accounts of their wonderful Christ.

They were already familiar with the writings of Luke the physician. Many had read the stories of John Mark, a cousin of Barnabas and spiritual son of Peter. They were also aware of the account of Matthew, who at the time was the only apostle to have written a Gospel of Jesus' life and works.

But there was something about the way John told his stories of Jesus. With eyes misting over, he would talk in a quivering voice about his beloved Master, revealing intimate details not captured in the other accounts. The church could not get enough of this storytelling. Over and over, they would implore John to tell the stories all over again.

After repeatedly hearing these stories, the elders of Ephesus came to John and asked him to write his personal memoirs of the Messiah. John resisted because he did not see the reason for this. Three accounts were already powerfully written and circulating among the followers of Jesus. Why should he add another? What could he add? But the elders of Ephesus persisted in their request. Having listened repeatedly to the stories of John, they knew that his gospel story would capture the person and words of Jesus in a totally different way from the other biographers.

93

Apparently after a time of fasting and praying with the elders, John finally consented. Sitting down with his personal scribe, he let his mind roam freely over the last 60 amazing years. His heart warmed as he thought of the early days of the Church. But thinking further back to those last emotion-laden days with Jesus, he was almost overwhelmed with grief.

He remembered Jesus' tender talks with the disciples as He attempted to prepare them for His death. He recalled the horror of His awful crucifixion and the crushing pain Jesus must have felt at the disciples' many failures. Then Christ was gone. They were lost, devastated, and in shock. Then came the unbelievably great joy flooding their hearts as the reality of the resurrection fell upon them.

Now the Lord would take His rightful place as Messiah and sweep the world free of sin and suffering. But then followed the bewilderment of His announcement that He was not going to stay. He had to return home. His last words were about the one He would send—one like Him, who would be with them always—an eternal Presence.

John remembered descending from the mountaintop where Jesus had left for home. He and the other disciples made their way to the Upper Room where they had gathered for that last meal with Him. In his thoughts, John reminisced about that last meal with Jesus. But in reality he was among 120 souls huddled together waiting for what Jesus called "the promise of the Father." No one knew what would happen. As they prayed, they wondered what it would be like when He came. Jesus had said that the Spirit would be just like Him and somehow He would be with each one at all times.

And then it happened—*a spiritual energy* swept into the room, and everyone felt the sudden rush of an irresistible power as it invaded their inner beings. In the blink of an eye, they all were enveloped in a *Presence* that was, well, very familiar.

The Presence gave them new hope and confidence as it filled the emptiness in their hearts. They realized that alien words were beginning to form in their minds. What were these strange tongues flowing from their lips? Before they knew it, in an exhilaration of pure joy, they stumbled out into the streets. Under the influence of this holy elixir, they uttered strange words that attracted the attention of the surrounding people. Unaware, they were passionately communicating the world-shaking message of a Jewish Messiah named Jesus in each person's mother tongue.

They went on to proclaim that the need for religious rituals of animal sacrifices had ended, and now forgiveness was freely available to all who would trust this Man who had come down from heaven. Right there at that moment thousands responded. In the days to come many more thousands would pour into the Church. The Good News spread.

A Trip Down Memory Lane

So many memories. John had watched this fledgling, primitive church emerge and spread slowly throughout the Roman Empire. Churches were raised up all over Asia Minor. With the rise of Paul's ministry, the Church was being established as a loving force to be reckoned with. But the light of those glorious days began to dim. The Roman sword was now oppressing the Church, and the Body of Christ was losing many of its finest members to the fires of martyrdom.

Almost all of the apostles were gone. For a moment, time stopped for John. A deep loneliness gripped the old man's soul. All of his longtime companions were gone, and he was ready to join them. Only one task remained: He must write his story.

How should he start? He wanted this account to be different, not just a biography. He so wanted to be able to do justice to the passion and power of his beloved Friend. His thoughts now were fully engaged. His mind began to pick up speed as it raced back in time. Like a video recorder on rewind, the memories started passing before him.

He intended to go back to the day he met Jesus, but his mind involuntarily sped right past that point. He saw only a great darkness, like the void that existed before time. There was no sense of the Presence as he passed through the dark days of Israel when there was no prophet in the land to be found.

The scenes passing before him gradually cleared away the darkness as he began to see in his mind's eye the great prophets of old—Ezekiel, Isaiah, Jeremiah, Daniel, and others—fearlessly speaking the words of Yahweh. There was a stirring in his heart as their words penetrated his spirit. Standing as it were in their midst he felt that familiar Presence that was empowering their every move.

But then his thoughts began once more to move back—as though searching for some dimly held memory. He was unable to stop the mental rewinding as it kept going farther back through time. He was now being drawn back, witnessing the glorious and calamitous history of Israel. With pain he now viewed tragic images of a people in captivity, subjugated yet longing for the days of Solomon and David. The glory days. Those were the majestic times for the house of Israel—the temple, the priesthood, and the glory of the Presence.

His mind seemed to be racing out of control. Images of the exploits of Samuel, Samson, Joshua, and even the great patriarch Moses passed steadily before him.

All of sudden, something familiar stopped his backward journey. He found himself on the ancient mountain, Mount Sinai. The whole mountain and its surroundings were crackling with a type of electricity, the ground was rumbling and shaking. Then he saw Moses on the top of the mountain begging God to allow His Presence to remain with the people. That is what caught John's attention! Although he wanted to linger, John found himself once more moving back in time.

Now he was seeing a people moving through a barren wilderness, people who were once slaves in the powerful kingdom of Egypt. But this was not what he had traveled back to see, so his movement continued back. He slowed somewhat as he came to the formative days of the Jewish nation—visions of Jacob, Isaac, and Abraham—but then he continued on.

Standing Before an Ancient Gate

John then felt the recorder decelerating, and the images began to slow. Finally all backward motion ceased. He found himself standing before an obviously ancient gate. His heart was pounding, and his body trembled as he stood there considering his next move. He found himself reaching out to the heavy, weathered gate and giving it a tentative push. To his amazement, it swung open wide.

Now he knew where he was. He had been drawn back to where it all began. He strode boldly through the gateway and found himself standing in the middle of the ancient garden. There a Presence was filling the place. It pulsated with an other-worldly reality. John knew it was here that Adam walked and talked face-to-face with God. As he looked around, he saw a tree standing in a clearing. Carved into its bark, to his amazement, he saw the words "God loves Adam."

All of a sudden he found himself enveloped in pure darkness. He could not see a thing. The darkness was overwhelming and frightening. Abruptly, a forceful, majestic Voice penetrated the darkness. John trembled uncontrollably as the very air around seemed to pulsate. Thunderous words exploded upon his ears: "Let there be light!"

Suddenly a brilliant light blast through the darkness, and John watched the birth of a virgin earth. The Word continued to speak, and with each sound the earth responded in obedience. Again John was overpowered by the Presence that seemed to surround him. *He knew that Presence.* He had been in that Presence before. It resurrected all the precious memories of his dearly loved Friend.

"Lord, is that You?" Still standing in the middle of the old garden, he now knew where he would begin his Gospel. A flash of light, the scene was gone, and he found himself back in his room. Now he was ready to write. He signaled to his disciple Papias[2] that he was ready to begin.

In the beginning was the Word, and the Word was with God, and the Word was God. He was in the beginning with God. All things came into being through Him, and apart from Him nothing came into being that has come into being.   John 1:1-3

Jesus—God's Word to Mankind

Jesus is God's first Word and last Word to man. It is so sad that in our day, men are more consumed with the Scriptures than they are with the Word of God. I understand how that can happen. I spent four years of my life dissecting the Bible. I thought that in the Scriptures I would find life. The reality is that all my studies did not lead me to Christ. In fact, looking back I see that they actually obscured Him. Learning only made me a spiritual glutton, with a bloated soul and starving spirit. My head was huge, but my heart was empty. I had a great deal of knowledge but so very little real experience of the spiritual.

I spent hours reading and memorizing Scriptures, and yet I never arrived at the truth I was seeking. I have to guard against anger when I think that the religious institutes of higher learning are most likely to teach us the word, rather than the Word. I can remember no classes in those four years that were about Jesus. He seemed to be referred to more as a means to an end—ministry.

Tragically, the Church has somehow failed to understand that the Bible is simply a guide—meant to lead us to the very experiences we seek. Our perceptions of the words of Scripture can sometimes obscure the pathway to the Word. I am not saying that the Scriptures do not have great value. The Bible can be a wonderful guide, opening doorways into spiritual discovery; but it must not be exalted to a higher position than the Word. When read with spiritual hunger, the Scriptures can feed our impoverished souls and shed light abroad in our inner darkness. It was while reading the Gospels over and over again that I discovered the Lord in a life-giving new way. But there was a difference in how I read in my later years than how I read in my earlier ones. I was guided by spiritual hunger, not motivated by seeking a good text to preach on, some "new" revelation to feed my spiritual pride.

God longs to speak to us in a way that we can feel, not just in our minds but with our whole beings. The final form of spiritual speech chosen by Father is a Man, not a book. It is in Jesus that we discover the "speaking God." He is Father's last Word to man. He is the Word man needs.

He is the Word, and He speaks the forgotten language of Eden. He comes among the children of men to resurrect the memory of that ancient home and tongue. Man lost the ability to speak the old language of Eden, but when Jesus spoke, He stirred long-buried memories. Men and women followed Him as sheep follow their shepherd because they recognized His voice deep within their souls. They knew that Voice.

Sitting mesmerized under this voice, people murmured to one another, "We have never heard a man speak like this!" The intonations of love and the articulation of acceptance reminded them of better times. Jesus was letting Heaven spell itself out in the ancient letters, taking man back to the Garden of Eden and stirring memories of glorious walks with Father.

It was glaringly clear that His way and words were far different from those of the rulers of Israel. These religious aristocrats always made the ways of God so difficult, if not impossible, and presented Him as harsh, demanding and to be feared. The simple people who felt inferior in the presence of these learned men wondered how they could ever hope to experience the transcendent and mysterious God.

Jesus, thankfully, did not speak in the dialect of those religious rulers. He was not addicted to theological language; His mission was to make the Good News simple enough for a child to understand. In anger, He attacked the shepherds of Israel for their abuse of Father's words. Not only did they not drink, they muddied the pure water of the Word so much that the sheep could not drink it. No more!

> Christ succeeded in making his point of view about life and the world prevail over our point of view, not by rhetoric or any of the normal forces of persuasion, but by himself. For the forces of persuasion, once they are spent, allow the previous pattern to re-establish itself. In the case of Christ we have a unique form of persuasion. It is like what happens when an error in our viewpoint is shown to us, and our mind reassembles around the truth that we have not seen. But it is unlike this process in that the truth that takes us over is not a correct proposition but a person.[3]   Sebastian Moore

Jesus' style and message were even different from his forerunner, John the Baptist. John's preaching was a heavy burden laden with the "old-time religion" threat of hellfire-and-brimstone. John lived in the desert. Jesus lived in the cities. John preached God's judgment. Jesus spoke tenderly of Father's love. John spent much time in fasting. Jesus spent much time in feasting. John's message was a funeral hymn. Jesus' words were a wedding song. The lost lambs came to John. Jesus went seeking the lost lambs. John Shea expressed it so well with these words:

> Jesus said
> We play dirges and do not mourn,

Frantic rock and do not freak out.
A new music must be heard
Which will drive us to dance
In a world wrung into flatness.
Tonight will we not all sleep
With one ear in dream
And one alert
For the crackling of the concrete.[4]

Loving Compassion and Healing Action

Like cracking concrete, men began to feel a life pushing its way up out of the hardness of their parched souls as they listened to the words of Jesus. The song of the Lamb was restoring hope in the hearts of God's people. Never had they experienced so much joy and acceptance as they felt in this Man's presence. His love was like a magnet, drawing all of Israel if it would let Him. His words flowed soothingly over their spirits as they lifted their shame. The people found themselves avoiding more and more the presence of their religious rulers but pursuing with desperation the loving presence of Jesus.

The religious rulers avoided the "unclean" in the Jewish community, but Jesus made them His friends. This attachment to the "common" man was a thorn in the side of the religious community. It was unsettling to their beloved positions. It exposed their hearts hardened by religious tradition and pride.

Jesus' passionate devotion to the poor did not go unnoticed by the surrounding populace. They streamed to Him in ever-growing numbers—the broken, the sick, the helpless, sinners, lunatics, demon-possessed, common folk, prostitutes, rebels, the disinherited, and the dispossessed. No one felt unwelcome. Throughout His earthly ministry, Jesus could never escape the crowds of people irresistibly drawn to His tenderness. His divine alliance of loving compassion and healing action drew the hopeful to Him day after day. There was no rest from the people who desperately followed Him wherever He went—but His shepherd's heart could not resist these poor, lost sheep.

And the blossoming of earth? One thing about him, however, he was never known to desert other people if they had trouble. When women were in tears, he stayed by their side. When old folks were lonely, he was with them quietly. It was nothing miraculous, but the sunken eyes overflowed with love more profound than a miracle. And regarding those who deserted him, those who betrayed him, not a word of resentment came to his lips. No matter what happened, he was a man of sorrows, and he prayed for nothing but their salvation.[5]   Shusaku Endo

On any given day you could find Him in places like the home of Simon the leper sharing a meal, or in the streets protecting a prostitute from the outraged attack of religious hypocrites, or walking the roadways in search of those who were lost and shunned by society. They pressed in all around Him. If only they could touch Him. If only they could get His attention. All throughout the land they had heard of the power of His touch and longed to experience that human-divine connection for themselves. The words of Jesus were empowered in the people's eyes by His actions. He didn't send the hypocritical message of the religious hierarchy, "Do as I say, not as I do!"

To the abiding rancor of the sanctimonious religious leaders, no self-preservative fear or religious inhibition prevented this Man from touching the defiled, as such were religiously defined. Lepers, prostitutes, the blind, the filthy, the crippled, the poor, and even the dead—He reached out to them with total compassion and gathered them to Himself. There, within His arms, they experienced the warmth of Heaven's love and received the healing and forgiveness their souls had so craved.

Jesus violated every conceivable tradition when it came to His associations with the marginalized of Jewish society. He infuriated the Pharisees with every compassionate touch. The Qumran community of the Essenes had an unconditional law: "No madman, or lunatic, or simpleton, or fool, no blind man, or maimed, or lame, or deaf man, and no minor shall enter the community.

"Jesus came to shatter these man-made laws with the vengeance of Heaven. It was these very rejected ones whom He had come to save. To the Pharisees He declared, 'But go and learn what this means, "I desire compassion, and not sacrifice," for I did not come to call the righteous, but sinners.' The Pharisees surrounded themselves with the rich, the wise, the educated, and the elite of society.

Jesus, conversely, surrounded Himself with the poor, the uneducated, the rejected, and the outcasts of society."[6]

> He had faith in the love of God. He was so moved by this love that wherever he saw the pitiable men and women of Galilee, he wanted to share their suffering. He could not think, since God was Love itself, that God would forsake these people. Yet no one could appreciate the mystery of God's love. The people by the Lake of Galilee eventually fell away from Jesus because they demanded material benefits rather than love, and therefore Jesus prayed earnestly to God for guidance to discern what best to do in this situation.[7]   Shusaku Endo

The Jesus Stories—Parables and Aphorisms

The words of Jesus, though simple in nature, had dramatic impact on the hearts of the listeners. His manner of delivery as much as the words themselves made the people receptive to His message. He spoke to them as an equal, not a superior speaking to inferiors. His stories were compelling and convicting, yet full of humor and compassion. His words seemed almost to compose some heavenly hymn that only those who had ears to hear could discern.

His actions were in perfect harmony with his words. No contradiction existed to create confusion or disappointment in those who followed Him. His life was a living symbol of the very words He spoke. He was a book read of all men. The love of the Father was fleshed out in His daily associations with the very lowest in the caste system of society and religion. He ate meals with the untouchables, defended the prostitutes, healed the afflicted and pursued the oppressed. And He didn't do this to make a statement. He preferred these people. He truly enjoyed their company. And they all in turn were at ease in the Jesus' presence; all, that is, but the religious leaders who despised this reversal of established order in their precious community.

Personally, I think they would have liked to be at some of those parties with Jesus, but they couldn't bear not being the guests of honor. It was unthinkable for them to have to take the lower seats with the riff raff.

Jesus' language was sprinkled with the poetic, the imaginative, the metaphorical. It disarmed and stirred curiosity in the hearers, opening their hearts without their even being aware. His powers of persuasion were honed by His ability to see beyond the ordinary. He loved the story method of getting His point across. Everyone loves a good story, and Jesus could tell a good story. He liked to end His stories with a twist that left the hearers walking away scratching their heads and thinking about them for many hours to come. His stories always had the goal, though not obvious to the hearer, of opening them up to the love of Father, who was always waiting in the wings.

> The aphorisms and parables of Jesus function in a partic-ular way: they are invitational forms of speech. Jesus used them to invite his hearers to see something they might not otherwise see. As evocative forms of speech, they tease the imagination into activity, suggest more than they say, and invite a transformation in perception.[8]
>
> Marcus Borg

Drawing pictures from their own familiar world, He arrested their minds, captured their imaginations, and opened them ever so gently to the stirrings of the ancient language deep within them. Jesus liked to put His listeners in almost every story He told, and by the way, you and I were there as well—*the least, the last, the little and the lost*. These were the objects of His loving attention in those stories He told.

> *"But many who are first will be **last**; and the last, first."*
> Matthew 19:30, emphasis added

> *"For the Son of Man has come to seek and to save that which was **lost**."*   Luke 19:10, emphasis added

> *"See that you do not despise one of these **little** ones, for I say to you that their angels in heaven continually see the face of My Father who is in heaven."*
> Matthew 18:10, emphasis added

> *And said to them, "Whoever receives this child in My name receives Me, and whoever receives Me receives*

*Him who sent Me; for the one who is **least** among all of you, this is the one who is great."*
Luke 9:48, emphasis added

Parables—Stories That Reveal the Heart

Parables were not a new form of communication. For many years they had been an accepted form of communicating spiritual reality. So what made Jesus' stories so different? In them He attacked the conventional wisdom of His day—the accepted psyche of the Jewish community. He reversed religious order, violated accepted social practices, and challenged the motivations of men's actions. In His stories He made the "bad guys" the "good guys" and the good guys were made the bad guys. The less honorable were made heroes in the stories of Jesus. The religious and the rich were always the villains.

The only judgment to be found in His stories was against the righteous and the rich. What was that judgment? They were judged by the Father's love. The compassion of their heavenly Father exposed the hypocrisy of their lives. Be careful what you wish for—the recognition of others, the riches of success, and the rewards of religion. In your attempts to move up the ladder you are actually descending. Pursuit of the first place will put you in the last place.

For most of my life I yearned for recognition. I threw myself into sports in high school because everyone knew that jocks were the BMOC (big men on campus). I decided after high school that I was going to go off to be trained for the ministry. Everyone knew the ministry was the place to be if you were looking to make points with God and man. Then came years of working for God, but I still didn't feel like I had found what I needed. I was afraid of anonymity.

Comparing myself to ministry people around me, I always felt like I came up short. (You do know that comparing is a stupid thing to do!)

I was in parachurch ministry in the early days, so when I returned to the United States from Mozambique, I decided the Church was where I'd find what I was looking for. And I did find it, well somewhat, but it didn't do it for me. What I didn't realize was that seeking the public place, rather than the private place, was leading me ever downward on the spiritual ladder. Only when I finally hit the bottom rung did I began to truly understand the truth of the Jesus stories. At the bottom, I was finally content because He was down there with me! What I was searching for was there all the time.

Well, Jesus challenged the established precepts upon which Jewish society was built. Hard work brings its rewards. Everyone gets what he deserves. The righteous will prosper. No rest for the wicked. Life is about rewards, requirements, judgments, and success. These precepts never prevailed in the stories of Jesus. They always ended up taking the brunt of the story. They were relics of the old ways of religion and just did not fit in the coming kingdom.

With His stories, Jesus created paradoxes and reversed religious rules: the broad way, enemies, rules, synagogue, religious ceremony, and the way less traveled; the internal over the external, relationships over knowledge, mercy over judgment, last before the first.

> Their main object is not to present the gospel, but to defend and vindicate it; they are controversial weapons against its critics and foes who are indignant that Jesus should declare that God cares about sinners, and who are particularly offended by Jesus' practice of eating with the despised.[9]   Joachim Jeremias

Forgiveness, compassion and mercy are the golden threads of the gospel that Jesus wove through His every story as proclamations of the Good News. To sinners He extended gentle invitations. Come to Him and receive water, come and eat to never hunger again, come receive forgiveness, come receive life, come follow Me. His critics, those who rejected Him, did not understand the gospel parables because Jesus gathered the despised around Him. Because they were expecting a day of wrath, the religious elite closed their hearts to the Good News Jesus was proclaiming in His stories. It was cheap grace. Sloppy agape. No one pleased God by simply being needy and willing. Otherwise, why had they spent their whole lives training for and toiling in the ministry. What was the use of unfaltering piety? The religious authorities had too good an opinion of themselves. To these men the gospel was an offense because it exposed them—their religiosity, hypocrisy and pride—and that was intolerable.

Drawing back the metaphoric curtain, Jesus revealed to the world the hidden language of God—the secret messages that unlock the gate of Heaven. " 'I will open My mouth in parables; I will utter things hidden since the foundation of the world' " (see Matt. 13:34-35). Understanding the secret meaning behind these words is at the very core of hearing God. This is why Jesus was so insistent that His apostles decipher His words and not just listen to the literal stories, encapsulating what He had to say. "And He said to them, 'Do you not understand this parable? How will you understand all the parables?' " (see Mark 4:13-14). Interpreting Scripture requires an understanding of spiritual language, the hidden truth that lies just beneath its surface.

The Penetrating Questions of Jesus

Jesus manifested a profound ability to ask the right question at the right time. He knew what lay in the dark corners of men's hearts. Through the use of questions He exposed the motivations of the hearers—not to shame but to heal them. Through the use of the poignant question, Jesus gently uncovered the realties of our inward life, the life seen by no one. But Jesus sees it. He knows what is in the heart of man because He has traveled the corridors of every man's heart. In fact, as many of us have discovered, sometimes to our chagrin, He sees our hearts better than we do. By the power of the query He turns the light on our inward parts.

The questions of Jesus were much different from the interrogations of the religious leaders:

> The Pharisees and their scribes began grumbling at His disciples, saying, "Why do you eat and drink with the tax-collectors and sinners?"   Luke 5:30

> But some of the Pharisees said, "Why do you do what is not lawful on the Sabbath?"   Luke 6:2

> "Is it lawful for us to pay taxes to Caesar, or not?"
> Luke 20:22

The questions of religious men are crafted that they might expose for the purpose of judging and condemning. In contrast, the questions of Jesus were specifically designed to reveal for the purpose of healing.

Most of us live in the external world rarely examining the inward way of the soul. We are more comfortable with the light turned off in our inner life because we know there are things buried we'd rather not have to confront. Questions force us to look inward, examining our motivations, fears, desires, and aspirations. Jesus had mastered the art of asking questions, and through the effective use of a question He opened a door to the inward world of man and led him to places rarely visited. Many are the questions Jesus posed to His enemies and followers. Lifted out of their ancient setting, these questions can still challenge us to look into our hearts.

> *"But what did you go out to see? A man dressed in soft clothing? Those who wear soft clothing are in kings' palaces!"*   Matthew 11:8

> *But Jesus answered the one who was telling Him and said, "Who is My mother and who are My brothers?"*   Matthew 12:48

> *He said to them, "But who do you say that I am?"*   Matthew 16:15

> *"For what will it profit a man if he gains the whole world and forfeits his soul? Or what will a man give in exchange for his soul?"*   Matthew 16:26

> *And He said to them, "Why are you afraid? Do you still have no faith?*   Mark 4:40

> *"How can you believe, when you receive glory from one another and you do not seek the glory that is from the one and only God?"*   John 5:44

> *"But if you do not believe his writings, how will you believe My words?"*   John 5:47

Questions such as these test our ability to look deeply at spiritual reality as they also force us to peer beneath the surface of life. They will also unlock the door to the ancient language. Our attempts to look for the answers to the questions and the struggle to express those answers open new pathways of personal and spiritual reality. We will either answer with a quick knee jerk religious reaction, or we will wait and let the question probe deeper into our inner self, shedding light on the things we have shoved down because we could not face them. If we allow the question to do its job, it will search us and reveal the hidden, broken places in our hearts that it may accomplish what Father intended.

I have meditated on the questions above and allowed them to work on me. I have been overwhelmed by the chord they struck within me. I thought I knew myself pretty well after the breaking experiences I have been through. But I discovered, to my dismay, that I still have hurtful, prideful ways that hinder me in my search for the ancient way. At times I wanted to give the right, religious answer but knew that there were other forces within me that contradicted the very answer I wanted to give. But in the struggle, Jesus has gently wooed me, embraced me and told me He is pleased with my progress. I have discovered my heart—the good, the bad and the ugly—and been lifted up in the arms of Father where I am continuing to find cleansing and healing.

There are three sets of questions that have had the greatest impact on me:

1.   And Jesus turned and saw them following, and said to them, "what do you seek?" They said to Him, "Rabbi (which translated means Teacher), where are You staying?" (John 1:38).

What do you seek? What a piercing, poignant question! The answer to that question unlocks the door of discovery to all that you desperately desire in your life. How will you answer it and how will that response be reflected in your life?

This question was posed to the two disciples of John the Baptist when they turned to follow Jesus after His baptism. Now why would He ask that question at that time? Remember, the questions of Jesus are asked to illumine our hearts, to make us really think. On tiptoe with anticipation, Jesus waits hoping, longing for the desired response. It wasn't a trick question. He wanted them to verbalize what they were seeking.

How would you answer that question? Don't think of a religious answer. Don't answer what you think He might want to hear. How does your heart answer? Are you seeking a spiritual favor, a gift? Are you looking for a powerful ministry bringing recognition? Are you pursuing a spiritual experience? What *are* you seeking?

It appears they didn't even have to think. Their answer was quick and decisive, for it had been in their hearts a long time, just waiting for the question to be asked. Formed out of a spiritual hunger that had been growing in their hearts for years, their answer was ready for the long-awaited One.

So as He stood waiting, in unison they sang out their response. "Where are you staying?" They weren't inviting Jesus into their world; they were looking to enter Jesus' world. They weren't seeking a revolution or a revival. They were not looking for a restoration or a new word from God. They were looking for an abiding place, and if they found it, that place would resolve all the issues of their heart.

Their response shines a searchlight on the Church in our days. Too often we are more interested in getting Jesus to come where we are than in finding out where He is. Oh, we're willing to travel halfway around the world if we hear there is a great move of God happening. But have we asked Him where He is staying? That could very well be different for each one of us. So it is critical that we ask Him where is He staying. Where can *we* find Him?

Smiling at their alacrity, Jesus also had His answer ready. He had looked into their hearts and was not surprised by their answer. His response was in the form of an invitation. Come and see. Jesus was inviting them home. They would find a home in the presence of Jesus—the home they had been looking for all of their lives.

Phillip then runs to get Nathaniel, urging him to 'come and see.' The woman at the well goes into her city and encourages the town folk to 'come and see.' This is an ancient invitation that still sounds from an ancient garden, calling us home. And it is the sound that needs to be resounded in our times. It is the call of the true evangelist!

> 2. And Jesus stopped and called them, and said, "What do you want Me to do for you?" (Matt. 20:32).

Another penetrating question sounds forth from the heart of the Son of man. It is a question looking for its answer. How do we answer that question? Probing our heart, the question asks if we know what we really want. Is it healing? Is it friendship? Do we want forgiveness for our wretchedness? Someone to care for us? Do we want a severed relationship restored? Whatever the answer given, Jesus has a loving response.

At the same time it is a question seeking to open a door. The heart of Jesus is ready to respond to whatever the answer. This is not just a curious question needing to understand man's desires or expose his selfish requests; it is a question seeking to respond to man's most intimate wants and needs. The question is birthed in the pool of heavenly love, longing to draw into its healing waters the sick, hopeless, helpless, broken, and lost.

The Lord cares deeply about the hidden desires of man. Pushing their way up through the disappointments and failures of life, these longings of our hearts are like a signal light searching the heavens for an answer—for someone to calm our troubled waters, heal our pain, and save our families. There is One who saw our S.O.S., and before it was ever signaled He and the Son of His love planned the rescue mission. That Son now asks you the question, "What do you want Me to do for you?"

3. So when He had washed their feet, and taken His garments and reclined at the table again, He said to them, "Do you know what I have done to you?" (John 13:12).

This last question may be the key to the whole ministry of Jesus as well as the true ministry of the Church. The answer to this question can unlock the secret codes of the ancient language of Eden. Here again we are confronted with a challenge—the challenge of familiarity. Having read these verses so many times we believe we understand them. We know the beginnings of Jesus' stories, and we know the ends, but have we caught the hidden meanings? We skim over the words in familiarity, and again and again chance missing the power of their true spiritual meaning. Do we really know what He did that night when He washed the disciples' feet? We are proud of ourselves when we make this a sacrament in our churches, but may have missed its true significance. It is easier to celebrate a sacrament than it is to walk in a truth.

The events of that evening became a sign for all future generations. Have you been taught the power of the towel? Jesus was leaving no room for doubt as He knelt at the feet of each disciple that servanthood was the calling He entrusted to us. As Jesus had served them, so He calls us to serve one another.

This call seems to have become lost in duty rosters of the Church. We have reversed the order. Far too often the focus of ministry and leadership is on being served rather than serving. Many are the sermons and the conferences teaching the people how to support their pastor or their elders. Rather than the shepherds caring for the sheep, we find sheep being fleeced for the sake of the ministry. The people sitting in the pews (or chairs) are being told by the pastor, the bishop, and every traveling minister who passes through to support the vision of the pastor and the church. We expect people to listen to our sermons but schedule an appointment here and there to hear what is on their hearts. Let's be honest; we are more concerned with our needs as ministers of the gospel than with the needs of those to whom we are to minister that gospel.

So what is this washing of the feet? Where is the value? Is it just a symbolic ritual?

By washing His friends' feet, Jesus was demonstrating that He came to cleanse and cover, not judge and condemn. This was to be the Kingdom way. Religion will always be the moral conscience for mankind—more concerned with exposing sin than with providing a covering for man's nakedness as Father did in the garden.

We live in a "dirty" world. There is much pollution soiling our souls—rejection, unforgiveness, betrayal, emotional trauma, and countless other diseases of the soul. Man strives, ineffectively, every way he can think of to remove the oily film of sin and shame that is smothering him. He has already discovered that the waters of religion do not remove the filth, but only spreads it.

The Son of man comes with a towel in one hand and a bowl in the other, tenderly offering to wash the muck from the feet of man. He stoops down at your feet, and caressing them in His hands, He lovingly looks at the caked grime encasing your feet. Religious men looking on want to condemn you for that filth. Jesus looks up to them, holds up His hand as if to shut their mouths, and then quietly returns to the job of cleaning and then covering your feet. With tears streaming down His cheeks, He washes until all is clean.

To its great loss, the Church has exchanged the towel for the sword. We seem more comfortable with the sword of judgment than with the towel of healing. The world is more aware of the judgmentalism of the Church than they are of the cleansing power of the Church. Men have heard our judging, condemning words but rarely have they heard words that offer to clean their dirty souls. It has always been easier to judge others from our ivory towers than to step down into the mire with them with the cleansing towel. We need to rediscover the cleansing towel and rediscover the example and call left to us by our Master.

Thus, Jesus asked them if they understood what He was doing. He loved these men and was prepared to serve them, even knowing that each one of them would deny Him in some way in the hours ahead. The memories of that night were etched on the hearts of the disciples as long as they lived. They went forth into the world as an army of servants. The weapon of choice for these soldiers: *the cleansing towel.*

The One who lived His life in service of others will return in that same spirit. He is certainly coming back as King, but it will be as a serving King. The Son of man has not lost His towel. When He returns He will come with the towel, girding Himself as He prepares to reign as a servant King. The invitation is clear. We are all called to sit at the table of the Father, where the Son will once again serve the children of His love. He is the "waiter" at the supper of the Lamb.

> *"Blessed are those slaves whom the master will find on the alert when he comes; truly I say to you, that he will gird himself to serve, and have them recline at the table, and will come up and wait on them."*   Luke 12:37

Endnotes

1. *The Life of Jesus*, Maurice Goguel, The MacMillan Company, New York, New York, 1953, p. 281.

2. A Vatican manuscript in the 9th century records that Papias, a disciple of John, was his scribe in the writing of his manuscript. *The Apostolic Fathers*, J.B. Lightfoot, Baker Books, Grand Rapids, Michigan, 1956, p. 271.

3. *God Is a New Language*, Sebastian Moore, The Newman Press, Westminster, Maryland, 1967, p. 119.

4. *The God Who Fell From Heaven*, John Shea, Thomas More Press, Chicago, 1992, p. 99.

5. *A Life of Jesus*, Shusaku Endo, Paulist Press, New Jersey, 1973, p. 173.

6. *The Lost Passions of Jesus*, Don Milam, Destiny Image Publishers, Shippensburg, Pennsylvania, 1999, pp. 123-124.

7. *A Life of Jesus*, Shusaku Endo, p. 73.

8. *Meeting Jesus for the First Time*, Marcus Borg, Harper Collins, San Francisco, 1995, pp. 70-71.

9. *Rediscovering the Parables*, Joachim Jeremias, SCM Press, New York, 1966, p. 98.

What an abyss is the grace of God! Who can measure its breadth? Who can fathom its depth? Like all the rest of the divine attributes, it is infinite. God is full of love, for "God is love."[1]

Charles Spurgeon

Grace is difficult to believe and difficult to accept. We want so desperately to believe that God loves unconditionally, yet we keep adding conditions. "Okay, fine," we say reluctantly, "but once we accept God's grace, we'd better get our act together. We had better be successful or we won't be worthy of his grace." We just cannot believe God can grace even our "failures."[2]

Michael Yaconelli

Grace is the reunion of life with life, the reconciliation of the self with itself. Grace is the acceptance of that which is rejected. Grace transforms fate into a meaningless destiny; it changes guilt into confidence and courage. There is something triumphant in the word "grace": in spite of the abounding of sin grace abounds much more.[3]

Paul Tillich

CHAPTER 7

THE GOSPEL ACCORDING TO GRACE

In 1976, I preached my first meaningful sermon on grace. The content of that sermon was drawn upon my self-enlightening experiences in a Communist prison in the country of Mozambique in southeast Africa. Mozambique had been the land of my prophetic dreams since I was a Bible college student. It was almost seven years before I would arrive there with my family ready to give my life for God on the mission field. Years later, my message that Sunday morning was not so much about what I did for God in that African nation, but what He did for and in me.

I already recounted the events of those three years in Africa, so I won't dwell on them, but just to note that it was there I took my first real baby steps in grace. Of course, I had always known the word, what Bible college student didn't? But that was probably the first time in my life that I actually had a face-to-face encounter with her. She became my daily companion in those prison days, strengthening me, carrying me and helping me through the dark days of fear.

Now after my ten uncertain months in that prison, I was back home with my family and the church that had supported and prayed for us throughout the time overseas. After some re-strengthening and regrouping time, my wife, Micki, and I felt ready to return to the work of the ministry. As part of the leadership in the church, we began once again to do what we loved most, working with people. We found ourselves especially drawn to those who were hurting and full of questions about the presence of pain in this life. Our own recent experiences gave us a genuine base from which to minister grace, and not just words, to these precious people.

We became enamored with the house of God. We loved being servants in His house. It was great for a couple of years, but as time passed I began to have that old, familiar, anxious feeling that something was terribly wrong. I was working once again for God, with the hope that being a faithful son would enable me to ascend into the high places of God that I had heard so much about. I so longed to breathe the rarified air of spiritual reality, but seemed doomed to failure. The harder I tried to get the spiritual lift necessary to go higher, the more it seemed to elude me. I threw myself deeper into the work of the ministry, beating as hard as I could the wing of grace—a grace I knew as a power to enable me to work in the house of God.

I went to deeper-life and leadership conferences. I read more books. Being part of the discipleship movement now, I searched my heart to see where I might not be submissive to my spiritual authority. The continual frustration of my emotional and spiritual effort eventually left me devastated and spiritually drained. Beating the air frantically, I became more shaken in faith with each failed attempt at flight. The time finally came when I realized that I was actually drifting downward rather than soaring upward. My spirit gave up in abject discouragement, and I went into an immediate spiritual free fall.

The Two Wings of Grace

Father, who had been watching my lifelong struggle to fly higher, finally got my full attention so He could impart in me a revelation. The profound truth that burst upon my spirit was *grace has "two wings."* I finally was given the understanding of why I had been unable to ascend into the high places of Father. I was flying with one wing. That single wing could never give me the lift needed. Whoever said that religious people get the simple things?

Do you want to know what the two wings of grace are? I'll tell you what Father told me. They are God's empowering presence and His unconditional, unqualified, unlimited love. No wonder I had never achieved the spiritual flight I had so longed for. I was experientially ignorant of Father's love. Oh, I knew His love doctrinally, but doctrine is a cold, lifeless tenet. My life had been defined by ministry, never by the spiritual reality of Father's love that His Son so passionately declared.

I had tried so hard to be a good servant in the house of the Lord, but I realized that I had never really gotten to know the Lord of the house. I had been a worker in His fields, but never experienced the unspeakable delights of being in His bridal chamber. In Bible college I had been taught the Word, but I had never let the Word teach me. I had learned to obey the voice of man, but had not learned to hear the voice of Father. I was more comfortable in the holy place doing my priestly duties than I was in stepping into the most holy place to behold His glory. I had always heard of those inward places—the bridal chamber, most holy place, Father's throne room. But I think I was afraid to look for those places of intimacy because I subconsciously felt that if I found and entered them, I would be met by judgment rather than the love I so craved.

Sitting there in my living room that morning, I felt as though waves of love were washing over me. This was Father's love? Amazing! So this was what I had been missing my whole life! The eyes of my heart were finally opened to the blazing reality of what I had always espoused. What really undid me was the realization that I was probably in the most unworthy place of my life—no longer in the ministry—just a painter who occasionally spent some hours after work putting down some beers with the guys. How could this be? Why now? I felt Him say, *"Why not now?"*

That was my introduction to the scandal of God's love. He gives it to whomever He wishes, whenever He wishes. And the truth is, He *already* gave it to *all* men in the person of His Son. Jesus came and wore our clothes and our flesh as a living embodiment of the love that He and His Father have had for us since before the beginning of time.

All those years I was laboring away in His fields and in His house, desperately hoping to please Him so He might love me, and I discovered that I was already home free. I didn't have to—in fact, I couldn't—do anything to win that love because it was already mine. Unconditional, unearned, undeserved love. As one of my favorite writers, Robert Farrar Capon, likes to say, *God won't stop telling us how good we are, but we won't shut up long enough to trust His judgment.* He reaches out to gather us into His arms, but we keep turning away to pick up another task we can perform in an attempt to earn His love. This is what religion has done to us, by the way.

Brennan Manning has really helped fix this concept in my soul. He emphatically declares that *there is nothing you can do to make God love you more and nothing you can do to make Him love you less.* The world has a saying: If it looks too good to be true, it is too good to be true! I'm sure you've discovered as I have, that that is a *true* statement—most of the time. But in the spirit realm, it has no validity. In Capon's words:

> The Scriptures make it clear that the world goes home to the Father by pull alone—by the Father's delight in a beloved Son who draws all to himself in his death. The abiding presence of the gift does not depend on anyone's faith but on the Giver.[4]

I felt that I was hearing the sweet refrains of some new melody that didn't sound like anything I had ever heard before—not in Bible school, not in church, not in ministry, not on the mission field, and not even in prison. I felt as though I had been trying to dance to the beat of a different drummer, always out of step. And what I was now hearing sounded more like a love song, and my feet were trying out unfamiliar dance steps.

Why do I call this scandalous love? I have to give credit where credit is due. I first heard those words in my feasting on the books of both Robert Farrar Capon and Brennan Manning. And when I read them, my spirit leaped and began doing cartwheels, I think. All I had to do to verify their conclusion was go to the stories of Jesus about the prodigal son and the workers in the vineyard. These are scandalous stories! You won't find tough love in the story of the prodigal, and you won't find men getting what they deserve in the vineyard story. What you will find is an outrageous, one might even say, unfair God.

He doesn't do the expected or the fair thing. Isn't that outrageous?

He freely forgives because His love won't let Him do otherwise. He gives men what *He* says is fair and just, not what *they* think it should be. What do you do with a God like that? If you're like me, you just throw yourself into His arms and say: "Thank you, Abba! Thank you!"

So over the last few years, I have been testing the power in my wings of grace. And I am finally getting that spiritual lift I so wanted. The view from up high is exhilarating! His scandalous, outrageous love and His empowering presence have changed my whole view-point and purpose in life. Your *perspective* of life is determined by your *position* in life. Because I was now in a new position, my per-spective of the Christian life was radically changing.

I have to be honest here and admit it has not always been smooth sailing (or should I say soaring?). The vestiges of the old life of sweat and stress want to creep back in from time to time. I hear a small hissing voice say: "This is too easy, you fool! You *must* be deluded!" Then I fall back into the old thought patterns weight-ed with guilt and condemnation: "What *am* I doing to deserve this? Can Father really love me—plus nothing?" At those times, my spir-it senses Him quietly entering the living room of my heart, sitting down in His favorite chair, and looking me in the eye as He says: "Son, I really love you! Let's just hang out a bit." Then I am undone all over again. The old religious conditioning is very strong and has a powerful attraction. It is only continuous exposure to the irre-sistible love of Father that keeps me from losing my way.

Amazing Grace, How Sweet the Sound

The prophets of old who lived under the law caught small glimmers from time to time of the grace that was coming. They would, in the spirit, step over the threshold between time and eter-nity and behold wonders of an age to come.

Some of them, I believe, saw in the spirit a Man walk onto the stage of Israel, speaking and doing things that left them reeling. As they sat down to write these wondrous, often baffling things, they groped for words to capture for others the impact of this coming One. I don't know if the word grace was part of their vocabulary in those ancient times, nevertheless they bore witness to it powerfully. The coming Messiah they all caught a glimpse of was going to bring a marvelous gift, not just for the people of Israel, but for the na-tions. That gift was grace.

> *As to this salvation, the prophets who prophesied of the grace that would come to you made careful search and inquiries.*   1 Peter 1:10

What was this grace they were speaking of? It was the grace to be found in the Lord Jesus. The prophets of old had watched "as through a glass dimly" as Jesus walked among men. They felt the shocking impact of the words He uttered—words of forgiveness, love, and mercy. These were words one did not associate with life under the law.

They were astounded by the magnitude of the coming change in the established order of the Jewish faith. Men would live under the majestic covering of love instead of under the spirit-numbing yoke of the law? The lion would lie down with the lamb? The prophetic accounts are rich with descriptive words of the things they saw.

It is essential that we understand these things, though the evidence of their prophetic insights cannot be found in words alone, but first and foremost in our personal experiences with the grace they foretold. Experiences in the truth must be wedded with explanations of the truth and love must reign supreme. Now abides faith, hope and love, but the greatest of these is love. The grace we all long to experience is found in the scandalous, spontaneous love of the Son that He enjoys with His and our Father. Grace must first be realized in the unshakeable conviction of the loving kindness of God toward you and me before it can be lived out in our experience. We cannot truly love others until we first are deeply convinced that we are loved.

God's grace is the dialect of the ancient language of Eden. The Father loved His son, Adam, before he was even self-aware, and He loved him as passionately after he broke covenant and sinned. God's grace was the very atmosphere in which the original man lived, moved and had his being. It never wavered, not even when Adam was escorted through the gates of the garden, and they slammed shut behind him. It followed him all the days of his life, just as it has every man, woman, and child who has walked upon this earth.

Amazing grace, how sweet the sound!

The Missing Jewel of the Church

Grace somewhere along the way became the missing jewel of the church. Though very much alive and well, grace has become obscured by rites and rituals. It is no longer the majestic song of the twice-born. It is still given lip service as the means by which we are born again, but then it is laid aside as having done its duty. Now the mantra is, "We owe, we owe, so off to work we go!"

We use the word in our religious and even everyday conversations, but not in its truest sense. I remember early on, hearing it explained as: God's **R**iches **A**t **C**hrist's **E**xpense. That's catchy! But what does it mean to us, the children of the Kingdom? To me, it has become one of those meaningless clichés.

I fear that it has simply become an overused word we have gutted of all spiritual reality. If we don't know what grace is, how will we know that it has two wings that will lift us above the manmade horizons, to the place of His glory?

Grace, amazing grace, is the defining difference between Christianity and every other religion. Judaism, Hinduism, Buddhism, Islam and so many others are founded upon the principle of works, whereby man aspires to see God. Man is taught that through human effort, he can climb the ladder to God. Although I love the writings of the mystics, too much of their writings focus on this effort to cleanse oneself before entering the presence of God. Entrance into the heavenly portals is believed to be dependent upon man's good works and moral living.

On the other hand, Jesus taught with authority of a new way. One doesn't clean himself up to get into the presence of Father; he is cleansed in the presence of Father. Jesus described it as a narrow way—narrow only because men refuse to believe it could be so *easy.* The road of human effort is a broad way because it is more acceptable to man's pride. Man's fallen soul wants to gain things— possession, wealth, even eternal life—by his own efforts. This was the sin of pride that caused the fall of the first man, and it hasn't grown any weaker since its manifestation in the garden. The first step of every man's spiritual life is taken by faith empowered by grace. "Through whom also we have obtained our introduction by faith into this grace in which we stand; and we exult in hope of the glory of God" (Rom. 5:2).

But then coming under the influence of organized religion, we are seduced into continuing the journey by the performance of good works. The apostle Paul mourned this as he watched men and women he had birthed into the Kingdom slowly returning to the old ways of religion. "Having begun by the Spirit, are you now being perfected by the flesh [human effort]?" (Gal. 3:3).

Religion perpetuates this false gospel through its constant haranguing of God's people with the lash of guilt. "You're not doing enough. Why did you miss that meeting? Why won't you teach a class?" The gospel of grace has subtly but steadily been transformed into a gospel of good works. The Church grades a person's spirituality by his church performance as opposed to his passion for Christ. He gets a good grade if he prays, goes to church, tithes, witnesses and does other spiritual exercises. The Church graders seem to have forgotten Jesus' words that it is not what goes into a man that defiles him, but what comes out.

But let me put in a word here on behalf of church leaders. Understand, they, too, are graded. They are graded by their boards, their people, their denominational headquarters. From the time they are assigned their first church to pastor, they are on a religious ladder, and any leader worth his salt, will be scaling it. If you pastor the same church for too many years, you haven't succeeded. You should always be moving on to bigger churches. Or if you're an independent pastor, you are graded on the formula of "membership divided by years served equals..." If your church membership isn't above a certain number, you fail. If you aren't on the short list of national conference speakers, you fail. If you aren't living like "a king's kid," you fail. You get the picture!

I don't think we would be doing damage to the Scriptures to take and transliterate the story Jesus told of the man finding a treasure in a field and selling all he has to buy the field. I know Jesus was speaking of the Kingdom, but I believe we can look at that treasure as being grace that has been lost as centuries passed, with the soil of religion being continually thrown over it until it lay covered and forgotten. It is time for the Church to sell all that it possesses to go buy that field, dig up that treasure, brush it off, and restore it to its rightful place of prominence in the gospel. Without grace, the Church has no message or relevance to the world.

Grace—The Power of a Holy Life

So what shall we say to this message of grace? Does it give one a blank check to do whatever he pleases because he serves a merciful God? With Paul we say, God forbid! Grace simply reverses the order we have grown up with. Righteousness does not lead us to God's love. God's love leads us to righteousness. I do not work hard to get Father's love. I walk in righteousness and work for the Kingdom because I am loved by Father.

Let's get real here for a minute. I like to think about my kids, now all adults, to help wrap my mind and heart around this whole concept. Okay, I'm Father. Do I love them when they don't do everything I want them to just the way I want them to? Absolutely! Do I love them when I don't see or hear from them for days or weeks? You betcha! Do I love them when they "sin" against me or my "name"? Probably even more! When they are at their worst, my love rises up consuming my every thought as I seek ways to help them. Do you see where I'm going? Yet we can actually believe that a perfect, just, compassionate, long-suffering God could write His children off. God's grace can never, ever be exhausted toward His creation.

In another place Paul said, "But by the grace of God I am what I am, and His grace toward me did not prove vain; but I labored even more than all of them, yet not I, but the grace of God with me" (1 Cor. 15:10).

It was because of this empowering presence, discovered on the Damascus road, that Paul magnified the grace of God. He wrote to his young disciple, "It is God who is at work in you, both to will and to work for His good pleasure" (Phil. 2:13). This wise man knew that the love of Father was a power for righteousness' sake. He knew it in his experience, not just in his doctrine. Having been exposed to the mercy and love of the Lord, Paul found a mighty energy within him affecting his every word and action. Grace accomplished for Paul what the Law, that he kept perfectly by the way, could never do.

Maurice Goguel, the French theologian, put it this way, "The man who is pardoned by God, that is to say, the man who has experienced the Love of God, will love Him, and will therefore be capable of being inspired by His nature. This reverses the apparently normal and rational order of the relation between religion and moralism. Usually the faithful can only enter into contact with divinity if their hearts are pure. The nearer one is to holiness the nearer to God. In the thought of Jesus, on the contrary, the communion with God which is given with the pardon of sin is the principle of the moral life and its starting point."[5]

The diehard religious spirit cries that this is dangerous, sloppy agape or greasy grace. That is a very typical religious reaction. But that tells me those who make that appeal have never enjoyed grace! They simply refuse to believe it is that easy. It's the old, "It's too good to be true!" mentality. I have discovered, to my wonderment, that there actually are believers who cannot imagine living the Christian life without fences. It is frightening to them to have all that freedom. Why? Could it be because they have never been personally acquainted with grace and her irresistible attraction? They don't know that she's not going to take them by the hand and lead them into the paths of sin. They don't know that she *will* take them dancing up the steps of the throne and plop them on Father's lap!

Some go so far as to say they understand the need for talking about grace, but we must be careful not to take it too far. We must keep it balanced! Capon humorously points out that you can't balance the 500-pound gorilla of law and works by offering it a one-pound bunch of love bananas. What you have to do is get a 600-pound gorilla and drop it on the other end of the seesaw. *Then* you will see balance. I think I can safely say the Church has a long way to go before its message of grace is going to be taken to the extreme!

Tracking the Footprints of Grace

The early Church had no such fear of imbalance in the delicious Good News that they had tasted and witnessed. Grace was the great theme of the primitive Church. We're told that when Barnabas was sent to inspect the work of God in Antioch, he was amazed at what he saw. In his report back to Jerusalem, he reported that he had witnessed the grace of God. He saw, fleshed out in men and women, the inherent power in God's love to take a ragtag bunch of individuals and shape them into a family. A family bonded together in true unity that conformity to the law's myriad of rules, restrictions, and regulations had never succeeded in doing. Everywhere the apostles went, that unmerited grace swept away racial and social barriers, melding the peoples into one vibrant witness to the power of Father's love. Those who had never even heard of the Jewish Law were being changed by the power of a new law—the law of grace.

Paul was deeply aware that his very existence was a marvelous manifestation of that grace. He never completely forgot that he had been a ruthless enemy of this primitive Church, responsible for the death of many fine brothers and sisters he would never know this side of Heaven. Christ was the *subject* of his apostolic work, and grace was the *substance* of the superstructure being built on that sure foundation. With the humility of knowing what he was by the grace of God, Paul built carefully. His writings are saturated with the preeminence he placed on the grace of God.

> *But the free gift is not like the transgression. For if by the transgression of the one the many died, much more did the grace of God and the gift by the grace of the one Man, Jesus Christ, abound to the many.*   Romans 5:15

> *Through whom also we have obtained our introduction by faith into this grace in which we stand; and we exult in hope of the glory of God.*   Romans 5:2

> *But if it is by grace, it is no longer on the basis of works, otherwise grace is no longer grace.*   Romans 11:6

> *So that in the ages to come He might show the surpassing riches of His grace in kindness toward us in Christ Jesus.*
> Ephesians 2:7

> *For the grace of God has appeared, bringing salvation to all men.*   Titus 2:11

> *Therefore let us draw near with confidence to the throne of grace, so that we may receive mercy and find grace to help in time of need.*   Hebrews 4:16

As the Church moved into the second century, the message began to slowly drift into obscurity. Already in the time of Paul, the message of grace was being attacked, as was his authority and apostleship. His heart ached as he wrote, "I am amazed that you are so quickly deserting Him who called you by the grace of Christ, for a different gospel" (Gal. 1:6).

Oppressive persecution from the Romans and the Jews was dimming the light of the aging saint's hope as he watched the dangerous heresies of gnosticism and legalism begin to find acceptance by his children in the faith. In an effort to resist these forces, the Church turned inward, "circling the wagons." Defenses and bulwarks of theology and authoritarian rule of bishops were eventually constructed in an attempt to preserve the ancient truths.

The day theology was born, the light of spiritual passion, fired by the message of grace, began to be extinguished. The Church moved from proclaiming the gospel to redefining the gospel. Theology and legalism crept in and slowly, like dripping water, eroded her spiritual vitality. These theologies eventually created horrible separations in the Body of Christ, while legalism began to lay dreadful burdens upon the believers. God's people were being robbed of their glorious message, being taught that it was more important what they believed than *who* they believed.

The walls of doctrinal certitude and legalistic performance, while protecting them, were shutting out the very Presence that was the Church's life force. The Church, unwittingly, was exchanging the majesty of God's unmerited grace for the security of a religious system that was going to bind her up in a theological straightjacket. It is a good thing that none of the men who lived with and sat at the feet of the Master were around to see this travesty. Theology had destroyed the simplicity of the gospel, and legalism was sucking the very lifeblood out of the Body of Christ.

In his poem, *A Death in the Desert*, Robert Browning, the famous 19th century poet, imagines the last days and thoughts of the apostle John. In this classic poem, John in a melancholic moment begins to ponder the fate of the Church when the last apostle has passed away.

> If I live yet, it is for good, more love
> Through me to men: be nought but ashes here
> That keep awhile my semblance, who was John,
> Still, when they scatter, there is left on earth
> No one alive who knew (consider this!)
> Saw with his eyes and handled with his hands
> That which was from the first, the Word of Life.
> How will it be when none more saith "I saw"?[6]

His question is tragically answered in the succeeding generations, as Church leaders moved the Body of Christ ever farther from its emphasis on faith and experience to an emphasis on reason and theology.

Law was now ruling the Church once characterized by grace, and it was a tyrant. Flawless performance was being demanded, and severe punishment often was meted out for failure. The Church was falling into the black hole of human effort, where the glorious light of the grace of the Lord Jesus did not penetrate.

Explanations about God—Father, Son and Holy Spirit—superceded experiences with God. *The Father was now the one being locked out of the garden of man.* Tragically, in the end the Pharisees won the day! Legalism swallowed up grace.

On an encouraging note, down through the centuries, Heaven has had those who succeeded in breaking free from the web of the theological trap of manmade religion. Desperate souls, hearing echoes of Heaven's love song, awoke from the spell cast on God's people by the destroyer. Their voices still ring loud and clear to this very day.

Augustine was one of those voices speaking to us from the fourth century. Lifted from a life of moral depravity by the attractive pull of Jesus' outrageous love, he spoke compellingly on the grace and love of God. But at the same time, he was battling in his soul with the conflicting forces of intellectualism and spiritual passion. Feeling compelled in his inner man to defend the faith, he lost his moorings and began to drift from his original experiences with God. But he was never able to forget the life-altering power of that love. He was forever held under the sway of amazing grace.

> My deepest awareness of myself is that I am deeply loved
> by Jesus Christ and have done nothing to earn it or de-
> serve it.[7]   Augustine

Known as the prince of preachers, Charles Spurgeon often returned to the grand old theme of amazing grace.

> I think it well to turn a little to one side that I may ask my
> reader to observe adoringly the fountain-head of our sal-
> vation, which is the grace of God. "By grace are ye
> saved." Because God is gracious, therefore sinful men are
> forgiven, converted, purified, and saved. It is not because
> of anything in them, or that ever can be in them, that they
> are saved; but because of the boundless love, goodness,
> pity, compassion, mercy, and grace of God. Tarry a mo-
> ment, then, at the well-head. Behold the pure river of
> water of life, as it proceeds out of the throne of God and
> of the Lamb![8]   Charles Spurgeon

Paul Tillich, another master theologian born in Prussia in 1886, taught in Germany and stood against Nazism. Tillich was often attacked and defined by fundamentalists as a liberal theologian, but after reading his works, one cannot deny his love for Christ. Few evangelicals, however, were able to hear his heart beating in tune to the heart of the Father. His rich description of the power of grace could only have flowed from a soul that had basked in the sweet presence of that dazzling grace:

> Grace strikes us when we are in great pain and restlessness. It strikes us when we walk through the dark valley of a meaningless and empty life. It strikes us when, year after year, the longed-for perfection does not appear, when the old compulsions reign within us as they have for decades, when despair destroys all joy and courage. Sometimes at that moment a wave of light breaks into our darkness, and it is as though a great voice were saying: "You are accepted. You are accepted, accepted by that which is greater than you, and the name of which you do not know. Do not try to do anything, do not perform anything, do not intend anything. Simply accept the fact that you are accepted. If that happens to us, we experience grace.[9]   Paul Tillich

John Forbes Nash, the Nobel Peace Prize winner and central character in the movie *A Beautiful Mind*, shared a meaningful charge that his grade-school teacher leveled against him at an early age. She accused him of having "two handfuls of brain and only half a handful of heart"—a description that could apply to much of Christianity. All his life Nash struggled to realign those aspects of his character. The screenwriters made the following statement a part of his acceptance speech at the ceremony when he received the Nobel Prize, "I have always believed in numbers, but it is only in the *mysterious equations of love* that any logic can be found!"

Brennan Manning, a contemporary apostle of grace, has impacted thousands of us with his message of the splendid grandeur of God's love. Manning, a self-acknowledged alcoholic, exchanged the temporary comfort of alcohol for the abiding solace of the sweet wine of grace. His words reverberate with authenticity. If you are not familiar with his writings, I strongly encourage you to get his books and feed on them. They have been a great source of encouragement to Micki and me in our quest to relearn the ancient language of Eden.

Jesus comes not for the super-spiritual but for the wobbly
and the weak-kneed who know they don't have it all together, and who are not too proud to accept the handout
of amazing grace.[10]   Unknown source

Robert Farrar Capon, another of my personal contemporary favorite prophets of grace, has written a number of classic books on
the underestimated power and scandal of God's grace. These particular words have been burned into my soul:

The Reformation was a time when men went blind—
staggering drunk because they had discovered, in the
dusty basement of late medievalism, a whole cellarful of
1,500-year-old, 200-proof grace—bottle after bottle of
pure distillate of Scripture that would convince anyone
that God saves us single-handed. The word of the Gospel,
after all those centuries of believers trying to lift themselves into heaven by worrying about the perfection of
their own bootstraps, suddenly turned out to be a flat-out
announcement that the saved were home-free even before
they started. Grace was to be drunk neat: no water, no ice,
and certainly no ginger ale; neither goodness, nor bad-
ness, nor the flowers that bloom in the spring of your
super spirituality could be allowed to enter into the case.[11]

The message of grace will always be a thorn in the side of religious men. It is an outrage to those who feel the necessity of the
fences created by religion, and it infuriates the "older brothers"
among us. The grace of God is meant to bind God's people together
in a community of love, yet has throughout the history of the Church
been the source of sharp division. Grace is a scandal to the religious.

By grace are you saved and that not of yourselves!

Endnotes

1. *All of Grace*, Charles H. Spurgeon, www.ccel.org/s/spurgeon/grace/all_of_grace.txt.

2. *Dangerous Wonder*, Michael Yaconelli, Navpress, Colorado Springs, Colorado, 1998, p. 129.

3. *The Shaking of the Foundations*, Paul Tillich, Scribners, New York, 1948, p. 156.

4. *The Fingerprints of God,* Robert Farrar Capon, Eerdmans. Grand Rapids, Michigan, 2000, p. 38.

5. *The Life of Jesus*, Maurice Goguel, MacMillan, New York, 1954, pp. 561-562.

6. *A Death in the Desert*, Robert Browning, www.geocities.com/Athens/Troy/1787/robert2.html.

7. *The Ragamuffin Gospel*, Brennan Manning, Multnoma, Sisters, Oregon, 1990, p. 25.

8. *All of Grace*, Charles H. Spurgeon, www.ccel.org/s/spurgeon/grace/all_of_grace.txt.

9. *The Shaking of the Foundations*, Paul Tillich, pp. 161-162.

10. Unknown source.

11. *Between Noon and Three*, Robert Farrar Capon, Eerdmans, Grand Rapids, Michigan, 1997, pp. 109-110.

*There may have been created within you a genuine desire
to serve God, out of a sincere sense of gratitude to Christ
for dying for you; you may be impelled out of a sense of
duty as a Christian, to seek conformity to some pattern of
behavior that has been imposed upon you as the norm for
Christian living; you may be deeply moved by the need of
others around you, and holy ambitions may have been
stirred within your heart, to count for God; if, however,
all that has happened is that your sins have been forgiv-
en, because you have accepted Christ as the Savior who
died for you, leaving you since your conversion only with
those resources which you had before your conversion,
then you will have no alternative but to "Christianize"
the flesh and try to teach it to "behave" in such a way
that it will be godly. That is a sheer impossibility! The nature of the flesh never changes. No matter how you may
coerce it or conform it, it is rotten through and through,
even with a Bible under its arm, a check for missions in
its hand, and an evangelical look on its face.*[1]

Major Ian Thomas

*He has infinite power, boundless wisdom, indescribable
holiness, but to us the power, the wisdom, and the holiness come simply in the shape of love. But we have no
such help in understanding God's love of His creatures. It
is without parallel, without similitude. It is based upon
His own eternal goodness, which we do not understand.*[2]

Frederick William Faber

CHAPTER 8

THE OUTRAGE OF GRACE

In Matthew's Gospel account, Mary's pregnancy is described as happening "before they lived together." What an embarrassing statement for an upright man like Joseph! This scandalous situation immediately threw Joseph into a moral conundrum, an unsolvable circumstance. What would he do?

Should he expose her to the law, which he was committed to with all his heart, or should he find some other way more in line with the power of his love for her? John Shea calls Jesus the "embryonic troublemaker" because even in the womb Jesus is forcing man to face the issues of law and grace. Right there in Mary's womb He is creating a troubling situation for the righteous—and the trouble He causes finds its root in *the tension between what the law requires and what love demands.*

In his classic book on the life of Mary, the Jewish author, Sholem Asch, with literary genius, draws us into this tension between Joseph and the religious leaders.

> It was therefore with genuine and profound shock that he (Joseph) received the summons to appear before the court of Nazareth.
>
> "Joseph ben Jacob!" the rabbi began, swaying back and forth like a man praying, and clutching at the silky white strains of his beard. "Information has reached us concerning the maiden Miriam whom you have lately espoused. The matter troubles our hearts and cries aloud for clarification…" He paused, and the sway of his lean body seemed almost lost in the voluminous black folds of his gown. "For even if such things have occurred in the past— as we know from previous instances that have come to our ears—yet it is not our way in Galilee. But the act of

which I speak is permissible only if the bridegroom ad-
mits to having performed the deed in the order of marriage; but if not, not. Now therefore, I call on you Joseph
ben Jacob, to tell this court whether or not you have mar-
ried your bride, the said Miriam, in the order of cohabitation, and whether the child under her heart is of your
begetting."

Joseph returned no answer. His face turned ashen; he
closed his eyes that had bulged forward, and his long
chin dropped on his chest in a gesture of shame and de-
spondence. He did not see the angry glances of his
brother-in-law, Cleophas, and the priest, Hanina, who
occupied the side benches reserved for the bride's kin.
He did not notice the wan, haggard features of Reb Elimelech whose lined face seemed to have grown more
deeply furrowed during these last days. He forgot the
presence of the rabbi and his assistants and the head of
the synagogue, the venerable Reb Jochanan of the sons of
Issachar, who was a member of the court. He did not even
hear the suppressed muttering of the congregation, which
occupied the rear benches of the court and thronged in at
the doorway. Nor did he see the faces of the women and
young girls that looked in through the open casements of
the courtroom. He seemed to have collapsed under the
unexpected blow; his very body had been drained from it;
and he said nothing.

For several minutes the entire court, crowded as it was,
joined in the silence. Every man stopped his breath to
hear how the young stranger would meet the accusation
made against him. But Joseph still said nothing.

"Silence is tantamount to confession," Reb Elimelech
said at last, anxious to put an end to the painful tension.
But the rabbi persisted:

"This matter is too grave to be dismissed on a mere
confession-by-silence," he said. "Joseph ben Jacob, I call
on you a second time, in the name of this just court, to declare before us whether or not you have consummated
your marriage by cohabitation, or whether, God forbid,

you are innocent in this matter and have not sired the child which your bride Miriam has under her heart."

The rabbi's words echoed away and left a deeper silence. Their full import settled on the consciousness of every man present, and fear crept through the hall as if the still air of the courtroom had been stirred by the wings of the angel of death. All knew what it would mean if Joseph were to deny his part in the affair, and all were tensed for his answer.

A long moan rent the silence and Joseph, sobbing, cried aloud: "Father in heaven, wilt Thou stand by to see the humbling of an innocent daughter in Israel!"

"What did he say? What did he say?" came the hushed whispering of the people.

"Explain your meaning, Joseph ben Jacob," said the rabbi.

"My meaning," said Joseph, "is this: what man or woman has poured this vile slander on my bride?"

For a moment the rabbi and his fellow judges sat stunned, as though the young man's accusation had been aimed at their heads. Then the bride's kinsmen rose in an uproar; Cleophas shot up like a man stung and shook a threatening fist at the defendant; close behind him was the priest, Hanina, gesticulating wildly. The murmur at the door swelled into a riot of confused, irate voices. But the rabbi raised his hand to silence the crowd and resumed in a quavering tone:

"Joseph ben Jacob! The Lord is witness that it was not from this court that the charge issued against your bride. Before we summoned you in this cause we received information which agitated our hearts. But we did not, God forbid, rest content with such information, for we took pains to search the matter out and heard witnesses of unimpeachable integrity—many matrons and young girls who heard your bride, the maiden Miriam, confess herself with child. She called upon the Holy Name and offered thanks to God for the grace He had bestowed on her. At the well where she draws water in the mornings, and again after dusk, she has confided in her friends. And still we delayed proceedings until we had questioned women who are versed in these matters, and who declared before us that your bride, the maiden Miriam, was with child beyond the possibility of error. We see no cause to doubt the testimony of these witnesses. We, therefore, ask you for the third time to state publicly, before this assembled congregation whether or not the child which your bride, Miriam, carries in her womb is of your seed. If, God forbid, some other man fathered the child, you know the doom that hangs over your bride, over her mother's house, and over all of us in the sacred congregation. Joseph ben Jacob, cleanse the name of a daughter of David; soothe the troubled hearts of this community in Israel; I beg your confession!"

The congregation had averted their faces from Joseph. Every man kept his eyes fixed on the ground as though the danger to the life of Joseph's bride were their common peril. Joseph did not answer at once. Then, after an eternity of breathless waiting, he lifted up his head and, looking full at the rabbi, said in a loud ringing voice:

"I declare before this sacred congregation that my bride Miriam, the daughter of Hanan, is chaste and without taint. She is innocent of all blame, for the guilt is mine. Deal with me now according to the Law."

His words broke the tension. The company relaxed as he ceased speaking and clenched fists were brandished at him from all sides. Behind him voices rose with anger and, above the general tumult, Cleophas, beside himself with rage, was heard to shriek:

"I'll have reparation from him! For the whole family I'll get damages from him!"

"What did I tell you?" shouted the priest. "Was there a want of bachelors in our town that we had to abandon the orphaned Miriam to this stranger who puts our noblest families to shame?"

Once more the rabbi silenced the crowd. He was breathing with relief, knowing that a terrible doom had passed over his congregation, and he turned in the direction of the bride's kinsmen, saying: "Our young friend Joseph ben Jacob has just told us that he has taken his bride to wife in a manner sanctified by the Torah and the Law of Moses and Israel. He has brought no shame upon the family and no one can claim satisfaction from him. From this day Miriam, Hanan's daughter, is his lawful wife and..." Here he turned to Joseph—"I pray your union will be blessed with joy and happiness." With that the rabbi stepped down to the bewildered Joseph and held out his hand to him. Lastly, he turned to the company and concluded with these words: "People of Nazareth! A new house has been built in Israel. Let us wish them good fortune without end."

Next to approach Joseph was Reb Elimelech: "As you know, Joseph, this has not been our way in Israel, and I had hoped my brother's daughter had deserved the marriage canopy. But with God's help your marriage will be blessed, and your wife will bear you sons to raise to learning and good deeds." And the old man turned homeward and left Joseph standing alone in the courtroom.[3]

A Troublemaker in Israel

Beginning in the womb of Mary, Jesus would continue to force men to make choices between the restrictions of legalism and the embrace of love. Will you be content with a spirituality that is derived from your human effort, or will you release yourself into the arms of a loving God? In Jesus, the Father's love was extending itself, offering a relationship founded on the benevolence of love, not the stringency of the law.

Many chose to accept that invitation, but for the religious rulers it was an offer they could not accept. In fact, let's be truthful, it is difficult for all of us. It is easier to expect that we must do something to earn this precious grace. I know that though I am reveling in the revelation of unmerited grace, I still feel the pull of law upon the strings of my soul. Surely, there is something I must do to continue to enjoy the presence of my sweet Lord. Maybe, this really is too easy!

The actions of Jesus were colored with a mercy unacceptable to the religious. His stories were insulting and offensive to their religious sensibilities. Understanding clearly the moral of His stories, they felt as though He was undressing them in front of the nation. They wore their religious clothing with great pride and hated Him for leaving them feeling naked. They did not understand that in their nakedness, like Adam, they would be most invincible. Jesus' message of grace and mercy was unraveling the cords of rules and regulations they had carefully wrapped around God's children. By His every word and action, Jesus repudiated everything they held dear.

> Severe laws were harshly enforced against the company of lepers. They were driven beyond the walls of the city and were forced to announce their coming with cries of "Unclean, unclean." Tax collectors were looked upon as a hateful blight on the Jewish culture; they were viewed as traitors to the Jewish cause. Women were relegated to the lowly role of servants in the male-dominated society. Publicans became the accepted catch-all term for sinners who transgressed the oppressive laws laid down by the religious elite.

> The spiritual community of Jesus' day had evolved into a caste society set up by the priestly aristocracy to eliminate the accessibility of the "defiled." The brotherhood of rabbis and priests constructed a wall that kept them safe from contamination by the dregs of the lower classes.[4]

God's grace has always been a scandal to religious men. Just ask Jonah. Jonah was a good Jew. He believed with all his soul in the absolutism of the law and in moralism. This spirit of elitism was the foundation of his life. It gave order and definition to his world. He was so glad he was not like others—the heathen. He considered himself a fire-and-brimstone prophet.

God gave Jonah a mandate to take a message to Nineveh that He was very angry with this people for their great wickedness. This should have been right up Jonah's alley—a chance to preach about an angry God. But you see, Jonah knew something. He knew that while Jehovah was holy, He was also merciful. So Jonah ran the other way.

God was forced to use extreme measures to get Jonah where He wanted him—in Nineveh, which was the capital of the Assyrian Empire. Jonah despised the Assyrinians. They were the heathen dogs who had swept across Israel pillaging and killing all along the way. They should be judged by God's wrath for having touched His chosen people. But he had a sneaking feeling that God was just itching to touch these heathen with His love, and cover them with His grace. Jonah wanted nothing to do with this mission. He says:

> *"Therefore, in order to forestall this I fled to Tarshish, for I knew that You are a gracious and compassionate God, slow to anger and abundant in lovingkindness, and one who relents concerning calamity.*   Jonah 4:2

Jonah was not lacking in spiritual perception. In fact, he was very perceptive. While he personally felt more comfortable with Jehovah, the thundering God, he was aware somewhere deep inside that there was another side to this One he served.

So this call to Nineveh created quite an internal dilemma for Jonah. He didn't want God to go soft on him and repent of severely judging this people. He wanted Him to wipe them off the face of the earth. Not daring to run the risk of being an instrument of mercy, he ran. He would rather camp out in the belly of a whale than be that.

Not much has changed since then; mercy is not as palatable to religious men as judgment. There is a road less traveled, and blessed are those who take that path of mercy. It leads straight to Father's heart.

Tearing Down the Fences of Legalism

The Pharisees had constructed more than 600 laws to "fence in" the righteous, and would probably have added more if they could have come up with them. Now this religious fence, or should we say palisade, was under direct assault by the man of grace. Nothing Jesus did made any sense to these religious leaders who defined everything by the Law of Moses. He had certainly upset the apple cart of their whole treasured religious system. They took it personally and wanted nothing more than to be rid of this troublemaker. They had lived under a schoolmaster of laws, precepts, and rules their whole lives and believed that chaos would reign on earth if this fence were removed.

The religious authorities were paranoid. They believed this rabble-rouser was deliberately trying to undermine them in the eyes of the people. For instance, the shepherd principle that Jesus taught was in direct contradiction to the concept held by Caiaphas, the high priest. Caiaphas advocated that it was best that one man should die for the people, so that the whole nation should not perish (see John 11:50). (He was simply making a statement of fact as he saw it, but it was really a prophetic word of Jesus' end.) In the minds of religious zealots every man is expendable in order to preserve the establishment. This principle has gotten a lot of good men killed through the years. Protect the system at all cost. No life is too precious to be preserved if it threatens the religious hierarchy. This principle was true in Jesus' day, and unfortunately it is still true today.

In stark contrast to this insensitive tenet, the shepherd principle as taught by Jesus elevates the value of the individual to being of prime importance. He declared that the shepherd—a true shepherd—would leave the flock, the ninety and nine, and go search for that one lost, foolish sheep till it was found. Because not many of us today tend sheep, we might not realize just what a shock this was to the people of that day. No sane shepherd would endanger his whole flock, leaving them unprotected, for one sheep! On top of all else, it was bad business sense.

For the Great Shepherd, no man or woman is expendable. Every life is precious beyond words. Yet, incongruously, on a certain level Jesus was in basic agreement with Caiaphas. His own life was expendable for the good of the many! After all, that was the purpose of His mission on earth. By giving His life, He was going to bring mankind back to the garden, to the tree of life.

> Jesus loves us as we are, and not as we should be, since none of us is as we should be...He offers himself to each of us as a companion for the journey, as a friend who is patient with us, kind, never rude, quick to forgive, and whose love keeps no score of wrongs.[5]
>
> Brennan Manning

Religious systems and churches often start out with caring for the individual but end up working to preserve their systems and protect their positions. Jesus saw right through their diseased institutions and identified the malady. The priests and leaders were living off the sheep, not for the sheep. Christ's love compelled Him to expose and do battle against this deeply entrenched system if He could only rescue one soul from its clutches. He restored the dignity of the individual as He focused on the poor and despised "little ones."

Law and Grace and the Moral Majority

The Pharisees were quite happy that they were not like other men. They truly believed they were above reproach. They scrupulously kept the letter of the law, seemingly unaware there was a spirit of the law. If God was pleased with anyone, they knew it had to be them. After all, they were religiously addicted to every jot and tittle of the law. How satisfying to be able to look down from their pinnacle of perfection upon those poor pitiful lesser beings! How they loved the deference paid them. When walking down a crowded street, people quickly moved out of their way. Entering a restaurant for refreshment, the owner always fawned over them giving them the best table in the house. Basking in the sunlight of the veneration of men, they lived out their sad, circumspect lives in the dark shadows of legalism. " 'For they love to stand and pray in the synagogues and on the street corners so that they may be seen by men' " (Matt. 6:5).

From the lofty security of their self-righteousness, they looked at the people as candidates to become their disciples, if found worthy. There was much jockeying among the scribes and Pharisees to have the largest following. They took time for a man if they thought he would join their "club," but when he was in, he became of little consequence. *Woe to you, scribes and Pharisees, hypocrites, because you travel about on sea and land to make one proselyte; and when he becomes one, you make him twice as much a son of hell as yourselves.* (See Matthew 23:15.) They were committed to growing their sects, and that meant imposing on others the binding regulations they themselves lived under. The imposition of this moralism upon others had become the albatross around the neck of the Jewish nation. They had become a people whose national identity was one of shame and fear far removed from their "glory day."

Jesus was able to pierce the *cleanliness* of their self-righteous facades, disquieting them as He exposed their superficiality and the emptiness of their hearts. We know that Jesus was never impressed with the exterior of a man's life. He had 20/20 vision, penetrating the pretentiousness of the flesh to see straight into the heart of man. To those who lived by legislated morality, this was frightening. Blinded to the real work their office prescribed—caring for the people of God and drawing them back to Him—these religious men laid heavy burdens on men. Forsaking the message of grace, they misrepresented Father as a harsh, demanding taskmaster. In exposing the emptiness of their hearts, Jesus was attempting to remind them of the divine calling that was theirs.

Parading around on the human stage in moral finery will never attract men to Christ. This is a retreat back to the old ways of the Pharisees, and it didn't work for them. In our efforts to impose our doctrines of morality on men we will simply drive them off. The *moral majority* is a 2,000-year-old failed experiment. It didn't work in the times of Jesus, and it has failed in our time. Rather than attempting to create an imperious army of moralists, the Church should be raising up a peace corps that will get down in the dirt and the mire of a nitty-gritty life and extend grace rations to the spiritually starving.

The apostle Paul joined in the battle that raged between the forces of law and grace. As a religious man with a pedigree that was the envy of many, his life was turned upside down when it collided with the grace of God. All the hard-earned religious training he had gone through went right out the window, and he was left with just one message—grace, grace, marvelous grace. Having lived a regimented life under the condemning sword of the law, he was like a new creature after his watershed experience with the amazing grace of a loving, forgiving Father.

Paul insisted that: *"By its very beauty, the Law of God condemns us all until, while we are still sinners, grace comes and liberates us from its curse without a single condition attached: no improvements demanded, no promises extorted—just the extravagant, outrageous, hilarious absurdity of free grace and dying love."*[6]

Legalism is a shameful stain on the soul of the Church. Why have we still not learned that the law has *never* been able to cure the sin-ridden heart nor heal the sick and broken soul of man? It has no

power to effect change. The law only binds people to a legalistic observance of its self-proclaimed prescriptions of what is good and
what is evil. The end result of that observance is death rather than
life. Perhaps, its most insidious effect is the pride of life. "Look at
me! Didn't I clean myself up nicely? Who needs grace when I know
what to do and I do it?" Then I begin to look with disdain at others
I see who aren't doing half as well. Do you get my point?

> The source of tragedy is that the good and the moral law
> are absolutely powerless to overcome evil and conquer
> the source of evil…Law denounces sin, limits it, but can-
> not conquer it.[7]   Nicolas Berdyaev

Christianity is all about the revelation of grace, not the imposition of law. Grace swallows up the law and makes herself its master. Whenever this order is reversed it has tragic results. Law
exposes our moral bankruptcy while grace reveals the lavish savings
account Jesus opened for us. Father's unconditional, unable-to-be-
earned love has laid up an inheritance for us that we will never be
able to exhaust. Law emphasizes what I must do, while grace ac-
knowledges what Jesus has already done.

Throughout the history of the Church, from the days of the
Book of Acts, there has been a never-ending battle between the
moral demands of the law and the free price tag of grace. The two
are in a life-and-death struggle for dominance in the life of the
Church. The outcome of this battle will ultimately determine the
fate of the Church and, so, the world. Grace and law cannot sleep in
the same bed together. They are incompatible lovers and should
never be forced to try to share the same house. Their goals and
methods are diametrically opposed to each other. Watchman Nee
persuasively explained the battle in this way:

> "Grace means that God does something for me; law
> means that I do something for God. God has a certain
> holy and righteous demand which He places on me: that
> is law. Now if law means that God requires something of
> me for its fulfillment, then deliverance from law means
> that He no longer requires that from me, but Himself pro-
> vides it. Law implies that God requires me to do some-
> thing for Him; deliverance from law implies that He
> exempts me from doing it, and that in grace He does it

Himself. I need do nothing for God: that is deliverance from law."[8]

The battle between law and grace has a long and bloody history. Men have fought, killed and been killed in its wars. Whole peoples have been wiped out in its path. It has been a *holy war.*

Subtly and silently the Christian community has been infiltrated with the need to perform. Men and women struggle daily to free themselves from the leadership and peer pressure to conform to rules and regulations. I have wept inside as I have had deeply wounded brothers and sisters tell me stories of their handling (or mishandling) by pastors, elders, home-group leaders, and church family. When they have stepped out tentatively in faith, daring to believe the Good News of grace, they have been rebuked, faced church "tribunals," been shunned, and then dropped from the "guest list" of fellowship events. I understand their confusion and pain because I walked the same road. It's called friendly fire. Only the military could have come up with that term!

As the Spirit of Jesus, which is all-encompassing grace, has been forced out of religious life, the vacuum has been filled with legalism, ritualism, and hierarchical rule. The ancient language so rich in grace can barely be heard over the chatter of religion filled with empty clichés. Because men could no longer hear the voice of God they chose to place their lives in the hands of religious men who would tell them what God was saying. The code replaced the life of the Spirit, the glory that rested upon the place where God and man used to meet.

Endnotes

1. Major Ian Thomas, www.mephibstreasury.com/Poem-Christianduty.htm.

2. *Creator and the Creature,* Frederick William Faber, Burns Oates & Washbourne, London, 1928, pp.132-133.

3. *Mary*, Sholem Asch, G.P. Putnam, New York, 1949, pp. 48-52.

4. *The Lost Passions of Jesus*, Don Milam, Destiny Image Publishers, Shippensburg, Pennsylvania, 1998, p. 120.

5. *The Signature of Jesus*, Brennan Manning, pp. 175-177.

6. *The Romance of the Word*, Robert Farrar Capon, Eerdmans, Grand Rapids, Michigan, 1995, p. 11.

7. *The Destiny of Man*, Nicolas Berdyaev, Harper Torchbooks, New York, 1960, pp. 84-85.

8. www.mephibstreasury.com/Poem-Slamlegalism.htm.

*By a mutually accepted convention, Christians, who nor-
mally deal in stocks and shares and politics and love and
friendship, talk together about salvation, the coming of
God, the love of God, and the love of neighbour, and so
forth. In this game they do not ask, "What does it all
mean really?" because they do not need to. They know the
rules. They know the language. And it is the old language,
a dead language.*[1]

Sebastian Moore

*How much happier you would be, how much more of you
there would be, if the hammer of a higher God could
smash your small cosmos, scattering the stars like span-
gles, and leave you in the open, free like other men to
look up as well as down! ...As long as you have mystery
you have health; when you destroy mystery you create
morbidity.*[2]

G.K. Chesterton

*History attests that religion and religious people tend to
be narrow. Instead of expanding our capacity for life, joy,
and mystery, religion often contradicts it. As systematic
theology advances, the sense of wonder declines. The
paradoxes, contradictions, and ambiguities of life are
codified, and God Himself is cribbed, cabined, and con-
fined within the pages of a leather-bound book.*[3]

Brennan Manning

CHAPTER 9

CLIQUES, CLICHÉS, AND THE RELIGIOUS CODE

Jesus is the light of the world, and that divine light shined most brightly during His earthly ministry and within the first-century Church. The ancient language of love, grace, and mercy Jesus introduced was a much-welcomed source of hope and joy to all who heard it. But sadly, even in those glory days of the primitive Church, a deadly infection already had set in to poison the glorious content of the ancient language. A virulent virus of judgmentalism, legalism, and intellectualism was festering beneath the surface of the message of grace.

The heavenly syntax of the language of Eden—in its original, God-breathed purpose as a way for man and God to communicate their passion and wonder to each other and the world—once more began to be tainted. As in the beginning, man again began to prefer the tree of knowledge over the tree of life. His hunger for knowledge, whether it contained life or not, eventually spawned a religious code.

The specter of this religious code has cast a dark shadow across the face of Christianity for centuries. Upon closer inspection, we discover an intricate, concrete system erected upon a foundation of religious works and walled about with manmade authority. Though its first stone laid was the Cornerstone, the Church decided it could finish the building with no more help from Heaven. Men and women were seduced into the matrix of the code by a false sense of spirituality based upon biblical studies, theological degrees, and religious performance. Kind of sounds like the scribes and Pharisees, doesn't it?

The newly birthed believer begins his or her initiation into the code almost immediately. Just like a baby learns what the no-nos are and what makes mom and dad smile, so the new believer starts to learn from the Church what will make him accepted and what will cause him to lose favor. The religious code with its tentacles of repression, tradition, and religious appearance has undermined the force of the grace-full ancient language of Eden.

The machinery of religion shut down the power source of creativity and free expression, the one great gift God has given man. Too much of Christianity still lives in a "flat earth" mentality created by the evolution of religious jargon and hierarchical rule. Man-made religion secures the place of those initiated into the language and culture of the collective clique. Few realize there is a whole other spiritual dimension out there just waiting to be unlocked by adventurous spirits who see the hollow façade of religion and choose to look upward toward the Lord.

Life Within the Religious Code

The environs of this religious code blind its inhabitants to the true spiritual riches of the Kingdom of Heaven. Theological training centers produce leaders as if on an assembly line. They are given degrees qualifying them to explain what they have not experienced, speaking a dialect devoid of spirit and life. The code has substituted theological knowledge for personal relationship with the One who walked in Eden with our forefather. *Explanations* of the gospel have replaced *experiences* in the gospel; a dead language has taken the place of the ancient language. Such is the power of religion.

> As soon as religion has closed up "the east window of divine surprise," and is turned into a mechanism of habit, custom, and system, it is killed. The spring of joy which characterizes true religion has disappeared, and the heightening, propulsive tone has vanished. It may linger on as a vestigial superstition, or a semi-automatic performance, but it is live religion only so long as it issues from the centre of personal consciousness and has a throb of personal experience to it.[4]   Rufus Jones

Humanity weeps to hear the sweet sounds that once filled the garden of Father's delight, reminding them of the home that awaits them. But sadly, Heaven's symphony has been drowned out by the drumbeat of a martial mentality. Marching in locked step to the cadence of the code has almost destroyed the creative power of Christ's Body. The people Jesus died to redeem have been lulled into believing they cannot hear the Shepherd's voice for themselves, that they need His words interpreted for them by "anointed" leaders. They are made to feel foolish or worse yet, rebellious, if they dare to think they have heard from God. Conformity—in dress, speech, and beliefs—is almost demanded. The leader's vision is to be supported with their time, money, and effort, while their own dreams shrivel away in their beleaguered souls. Dreams, if repressed indefinitely, metastasize into cancerous feelings of hopelessness and disillusionment. Cynicism replaces hope, extinguishing the flames of spiritual passion that once burned brightly. People who endure repression of their hopes and dreams for an indefinite period eventually become listless and lifeless.

History is peppered with accounts of subjugated people rising up in a blaze of passionate revolt as they endeavored to throw off the unbearable chains of slavery. I believe with my whole heart that the Church is ripe for just such a revolution by the "palace peasants" who are soul-sick from feeding on husks doled out by their masters.

The Pillars of the Code

For us to return to the ancient garden of passionate love, we have to understand how we got into this fine mess. As the saying goes, those who do not learn from history are doomed to repeat it. This holds true for church history every bit as much as for world history. It is a well-recognized fact that every spiritual renewal eventually got swallowed up by the religious establishment—or it became the religious establishment. Oftentimes, the supporters of the past reformation become the persecutors of the new one. It is the nature of the code to reproduce its insidious life in every fresh, vital body it can find, sucking it dry of any grace and freedom it has enjoyed. It may start as a tiny seed, or as Jesus said, as a little yeast that in a short time leavens the whole loaf.

The house that God built has been repeatedly torn down and rebuilt into the image of man. This hellish reconstruction project has ruthlessly torn down the columns of scandalous grace, loving community, inspired creativity, and intimate spiritual experience.

The skyline of Christianity now has an unmistakably manmade look supported by the pillars of empty clichés, crusty customs, sanctimonious conduct and the rubberstamp of doctrinal correctness.

A gospel filled with irrelevant answers, hollow traditions, moral hypocrisy, and hardened hierarchies can hardly be considered an appropriate gift for a world starving for just "a little love and understanding." Jesus asked the rhetorical question, "What father would give his son a stone, when he asked for bread?" Is the Church guilty of this very thing? Men are crying for bread, and we give them a doctrinal system? Can this be reversed? "Can a leopard change her spots?" you might ask. I believe it can, but for this to happen we must identify the code, expose it to the light of day, and then purge it from our midst.

Creeds and Systematic Theology

Through the centuries theology slowly shifted the emphasis from the person of Christ to the *principle* of Christ. As the first- and second-century Church faced the onslaught of heresies and gnosticism, the church leaders chose to do battle with these forces on an intellectual basis. The light of the Spirit was replaced with the light of the intellect.

Many of the early church fathers, having been heavily influenced by Greek philosophy in their pre-Christ days, gradually introduced the Church to a new facet of spirituality—intellectualism (a devotion to the exercise of the intellect)—upon becoming leaders of the Way. Fighting the hordes of heresies coming at the Church from every quarter, they attempted to wage warfare in the spirit using manmade weapons. They forgot or ignored the apostle Paul's declaration that we are fighting principalities and powers in heavenly places. The pursuit of knowledge began to supercede spiritual revelation.

This trend toward rationalization and intellectualism reached its peak with the writings and influence of Thomas Aquinas in the 13th century. He set up universities to study theology, and these schools were steeped in rationalism. All of Aquinas' writings have the stamp of a "scholastic" approach to theology. His writings, heavily influenced by the writings of Aristotle, were "impersonal and monotone compared with Augustine, because their procedure is constantly analytic, with numerous divisions and subdivisions, with sharp distinctions of concepts and formal distinctions, with objections and answers, with all the means of grammar, dialectic and disputation."[5]

This approach to the gospel is in great contradistinction to the gospel of the apostles, who emphasized faith and revelation over reason and intellectual study. This shift is powerfully illustrated in the difference of emphasis between Augustine and Aquinas. Augustine emphasized, "I believe in order to know," while Aquinas reversed the order by saying, "I know in order to believe." This subtle shift meant that spiritual knowledge was now pursued through the power of the mind and human reasoning rather than faith and dependence on the Holy Spirit.

Again the tree of the knowledge of good and evil can be seen luring man away from his true source of strength—his relationship with the Father and dependence on the Holy Spirit

So the tide of intellectualism crested, sweeping over the Church, leaving in its wake a barren land stripped of life and passion. The devastating result was that the Church became more concerned with *what* people believed than in *whom* people believed. The church fathers labored and fought over exact wording, agreeing finally upon carefully constructed systems of doctrine that would be the bastion for the beleaguered Church. They presumed in their darkened minds that this system of beliefs would keep the house of God pure and united. So began conformity of thought and belief that came to be one of the central pillars of the code.

In the fourth century, the Roman emperor Constantine called for the first ecumenical councils of the Church. Though he had pretty much stopped the Roman persecutions of the Church, Constantine was no friend of the purposes of God. It was his goal in these synods to establish a universal basis of truth. By his mandate, the resolutions adopted at the Nicene council became imperial laws. The Church needed "a uniform 'ecumenical creed,' and this was to be the Church's law and imperial law for all the churches. He believed that only in this way could he ensure the unity of the empire under the slogan: one God—one emperor—one kingdom—one church—one faith.' "[6] The unity in the Church created by the Holy Spirit was now substituted with a unity created by doctrine.

This preoccupation with strict inarguable definitions of religious belief rather than enlightening by the Spirit actually obscured the path to God. By so strictly defining the indefinable God and the Christian walk, they deprived the Church of the power of the mystery. Preaching from the seat of the learned took the place of preaching from the lap of the Father. An obsession with the *letter* of the Scriptures took the place of the *life* contained in the Scriptures. The stripping away of mystery left the Church in a rigid, closed system at the mercy of man's will.

No one would deny the importance of studying the Scriptures, digging for the gems of truth scattered throughout, and accurately understanding the truth of the Scriptures. But to study for the primary purpose of learning truths leaves us feeding from the tree of knowledge, not the tree of life. I know, because that is what I did throughout my years in the ministry. I was always looking for some rare gem of revelation that hadn't been seen before, forgetting, to my own hurt, that the pearl of great price was right before my eyes.

Knowledge that is not grounded in a living, vibrant daily relationship with Him is dry and dead with no value or power. God, in the person of Jesus, emphatically declared that knowing the truth would set one free. Knowing Jesus, not doctrine, would set men free. He knew that man was always off searching some highway or byway for somebody or something that would free him from his pain. Why do we spend hours, months, and years studying "truths" when we have an open invitation to live in intimacy with the Truth? Traveling down roads of intellectualism and higher learning will only lead to more confusion, cynicism and, eventually, unbelief. Study of systematic theology may give an illusion of security, but it will never lead to that place that our souls cry out for—our home in His presence.

Idioms and Clichés of the Code

As the scaffolding of doctrinal correctness was being constructed, a new vocabulary was growing within the matrix of religious life. The idioms of theology were slowly but surely replacing the "sweet nothings" of the love language of Eden. This orthodoxy of church canon did damage to the simple life of the Church.

Man was once again eating from the tree of knowledge, progressively moving farther away from the foundation of the Church, which was genuine encounters with the living God. As believers gathered together, those meetings became times of instruction in theology. Instead of fellowship and sharing the joyous life each was experiencing, they grew accustomed to sitting quietly as one or two "leaders" stood before them, telling them God's plan as they saw it. The apostolic manner of preaching was reversed. Preachers, trained not in the wilderness or at the feet of the Master, spoke down to the people from their superior position of training and accreditation, rather than out of weakness and trembling such as Paul experienced.

> *And when I came to you, brethren, I did not come with superiority of speech or of wisdom, proclaiming to you the testimony of God. I was with you in weakness and in fear and in much trembling, and my message and my preaching were not in persuasive words of wisdom, but in demonstration of the Spirit and of power, so that your faith would not rest on the wisdom of men, but on the power of God.*   1 Corinthians 2:1-4

It was soon a recognized, though unspoken, part of the code that this teaching was not to be questioned, and it is possibly even more so today.

Some time ago, I was sitting in a church service listening to a guest speaker from another country who was welcomed to this particular church as an apostle whenever he was in the area. Throughout his preaching, I was struggling to keep my heart free from cynicism. I was listening to the same old guilt trip that I had heard from the pulpit since I was a kid and had, in fact, employed myself in later years. "Look what I'm doing for God! What are you doing?" It was all about works!

Just then, a teenage girl jumped out of her seat crying: "What about Jesus? What does all this have to do with Jesus?" I'm sure you can imagine the stunned silence that held the room in its grip. This could have been the Spirit Himself crying out for our attention. Having been around the block a couple of times, I had a pretty good idea what was going to happen, but hope springs eternal! One of the church authorities slipped out of his seat, walked over to the now crying girl, took her by the arm and quickly ushered her out of the room—and out of the building. The apostle went back to his preaching. What a lost opportunity!

As theology grew, it took on its own life, creating great divisions in the Body of Christ—divisions or cliques of denominationalism and intellectualism. Differences of opinion and doctrinal interpretation gave rise to denominations. Predestination, celebration of the Lord's Supper, methods of sanctification, baptism, modes of worship, spiritual gifts, eternal security—the divergence of opinions grew exponentially, further eating away at the unity of Christ's Church. This splintering of the Body became an added source of great sorrow in the heavenly realms. One could almost hear the sound of nature's groaning, increasing in an orchestrated crescendo, as they longed for the freedom of the sons of God. "Behold, how they love one another" was replaced with, "Behold, how they judge one another"— another breakdown of the syntax of the ancient language.

Clergy and Laity—New Divisions in the Body of Christ

Perhaps, even more destructive than the division into denominations was the secondary fissure that took place—the creation of a distinction between clergy and laity. Cliques were truly being set in place in the Church. Of course, there is no doubt in anyone's mind what the pecking order is in these cliques. The clergy have always been the elite, the inner circle. Whether this comes from having an alphabet after their names from elite schools of higher learning or from an actual call by the Spirit, only God truly knows. But the clergy is firmly established as the guardians and tutors of spiritual truth.

They are secure in their trappings of exclusivity because they are knowledgeable—in biblical languages, biblical criticism, and the weighty writings of historical theologians. They have the credentials, and that gives them the authority. The laity, on the other hand, are the poor unlearned "masses" expected to sit hour after hour, day after day, year after year, in gratitude and awe at the intellectual pearls dropping from the lips of the leaders.

I must sound pretty hardened, but I struggled for years in the system, trying to guard my heart from cynicism at the things I witnessed. My struggles began in my early days in a respected Bible college, which I attended with high ideals. I became initiated early in the code. As students we were expected to take copious notes in the classrooms. This, in itself, was not a problem for me. I loved it. But the fly in the ointment came when it was time to write papers for major grades. It didn't take long to learn that we got great grades if we regurgitated back to the professors their own thoughts and words. If anyone dared to think differently, to offer individualistic ideas from one's own study of the Scriptures, he or she was almost guaranteed a failing grade. There might as well have been a sign over each classroom door warning, "Free thinking not allowed." So the initiates into the code learn early: *conform or proceed at your own risk.*

Today's religious authority structure is much the same as in Jesus' day when religious leaders, whether consciously or unconsciously, made the people (the laity) feel inferior. The Jewish leaders were the keepers of the law and representatives of all truth. And now we see that same phenomenon in the modern church. The average believer must be taught the truth. They cannot be trusted to discover it for themselves. They do not have the necessary tools. They might interpret the Scriptures wrongly and end up down some side alley of heresy. The tools of the Spirit—discernment, revelation, prophecy, and spiritual insight—which are the inherent birthright of every child of God, are not enough. The code dictates that the tools of theology—textual criticism, and understanding the biblical languages and biblical interpretation—are necessary for rightly dividing the truth. "Behold how unlearned these men are" was replaced with "Behold how learned these men are."

Religion clouded the mysteries of Christ, as her high priests presumed to explain what they had not encountered. Intellectualism puffed men up, making them appear larger than they really were. This emphasis on academic Christianity contributed greatly to the ancient language being forgotten. The Church became a prisoner of her own theories and prejudices, her own code, rather than being a prisoner for Christ.

> He eludes all our words and categories. We cannot objectify or conceptualize Him. When we try, we fall immediately into contradiction.[7]   Frederick Ferre

The truth of the matter is, God eludes all our attempts to define Him. There are no words in the language of man to fully explain the majesty of His Being. He may appear, because of His elusiveness, to be a tame house cat we can keep in a cage, but He is in the reality of eternity a lion whose roar echoes down the corridors of time. He cannot be put in a box. My friend, Don Nori, likes to say He is God out of the box and God out of control. But religion is still obsessed with trying to get Him into that safe box.

> And the continuous statement of the fact without explanation causes a steady debasement in the value and meaningfulness of the statement...The concept of God with which we still operate is the focus of a religious experience that was once vital and is now being immobilized in lifeless jargon.[8]   Sebastian Moore

Clichés of the Collective Cliques

Empty clichés grown in the greenhouse of empty religion have always been a telltale mark of the code. A cliché, as defined by Webster, is a trite phrase or expression; a platitude, a tired phrase, hackneyed, stereotyped. Get the picture? A cliché is something that has lost originality, ingenuity, and impact by *long overuse.*

I'm sure I'm not alone in remembering in my childhood years the frightening power of cliques to intimidate the newcomer on the scene. There were the jocks, there were the really popular kids, there were the "brains," and so on. The inner circles of these cliques were surrounded by this mystical aura that lent them an air of invulnerability. They all seemed to have secret handshakes, mysterious passwords, and special rites. And they all had their catchphrases that effectively excluded nonmembers.

I'm an adult now, and I've discovered to my dismay that cliques and clichés are just as real in the grownup world. The Church is no exception. These clichés have emerged into buzzwords within the various cliques of Christianity.

Here are just a few: Jesus saves; enter the joy of the Lord; be led by the Spirit; do you know the Lord?; look to God in prayer; plead the blood; make a profession of faith; put it in the Lord's hands; ask Jesus into your heart; I have a burden for you; pray through; soul-winning; sanctification; predestination; under conviction; walking with the Lord; praise the Lord!

You could add many, many more, I'm sure. What do all these phrases really mean? Where did they come from? What relevance do they have to nonmembers of our cliques? Have they, in fact, successfully shut out those we call heathen? Is that, perhaps, their true intent?

It is no wonder why I was so ineffective while witnessing on the streets of Philadelphia. I was speaking a foreign language to those poor people I encountered. A language of clichés I had assimilated even in those early days of my ministry. I had no idea! I was given all these evangelism tools in my Bible college, but was missing the one tool I really needed. Why didn't I just talk to them about the scandalous love of the Son of God? I can answer that! *Because I didn't know it myself.*

We live our Christian lives on the surface of religion, fearing to plumb the depths of what lies beneath. What if there is nothing or no one there? We are terrified of the silence we might find there. Our conversations and attempts to introduce others to God often reflect the frightening reality of an empty life. Diving into the realm of the Spirit, the One Jesus promised, is the only way we will ever experience ourselves, yet alone introduce to *outsiders*, the richness of life—abundant life, we so crave. The circular process describes life in the form of two circles of life, the outer ring and the inner ring—and encourages man to plumb the depths of his inner life.

Most of us live life on the outer ring—our soul realm. This is the realm where our thoughts are hopelessly scrambled with concerns about our jobs, relationships, church activities and obligations, and diversions to deal with all the stress. Most of us, through all our religious indoctrination, were never even made aware of the inner ring—our spirit realm. This is where who we are really exists. We are a spirit, living in a body with a soul. We are spirit beings who rarely, if ever, delve deeper through contemplation and restful silence into our true identity as sons of the second Adam.

> Man has lost the power of knowing real being, has lost access to reality and been reduced to studying knowledge. And so in his pursuit of knowledge he is faced throughout with knowledge and not with being.[9]
>
> Nicolas Berdyaev

The Ministry and Corporate Christianity

Going back to church history, as the Greeks exerted their influence on the Church with their emphasis on wisdom, so the Romans shaped the growing Church with their emphasis on law and order. The Roman government was made up of senators, consuls, praetors, censors, tribunes, and so on. The Roman church took on the form of the culture in which it was birthed and existed. An intricate and complex governmental structure grew up with a pope, archbishops, cardinals, bishops, priests, and then pastors.

The development of this religious hierarchy was slow but steady. Fearing disorder and heresy in the Body of Christ, men felt the need to have imposed authority. What began as a positive desire to protect the Body from trouble inside and out eventually hardened into a rigid system with an obsession for control. Control is always the fruit of seeds of insecurity and self-preservation. Subtly, the bishops of the Church in its widespread existence became lords over its spiritual life rather than the Spirit—the final word, as it were. Submission to these bishops became a determining factor in the burgeoning growth and power of the Church. Ignatius, the bishop of Ephesus in the second century, did his part to set the stage for future generations to exist under ecclesiastical control. His writings are in shocking contradiction to the writings of Paul.

> "Do ye all follow the bishop, as Jesus Christ followed the Father. Let no man do aught of things, pertaining to the Church, apart from the bishop. Wheresoever the bishop shall appear, there let the people be; even as where Jesus may be, there is the universal Church. It is not lawful apart from the bishop either to baptize or to hold a love-feast; but whatsoever he shall approve, this is well-pleasing to God."[10]

Rather than being instruments wielded by the Spirit promoting spiritual development, the bishops attempted to control spiritual development. To protect the flock, religious leaders felt pressured to step in and establish religious order. And that was only the beginning. As the life of the Spirit was forced out, professional clergy took its place. The original apostles and prophets were replaced with bishops, cardinals, superintendents, priests, pastors, elders, and so on.

The forced labor camps of the religious community were conscripted to build a highway system upon which only the elite and the privileged could travel. Rather than leaders supporting the work of the ministry, the work of ministry became the means of support for Church leaders. Ministries used the "wool" of the flock to finance their own visions while the dreams of others remained in the barrel of unfulfilled reality. Thus was born a new profession—the ministry. Today it ranks right up there with doctors, lawyers, and politicians.

The essence of the Christian life steadily evolved from the supple wineskin of spontaneous, free flowing, Spirit-led worship and ministry into a rigid, brittle wineskin of organized, contrived, controlled, and rigid ritual and liturgy. The rule of the clergy over the laity nurtured passivity, effectively destroying spontaneity and creativity. This perversion of Father's design led to ongoing spiritual immaturity in the Body of Christ.

It is grievous when the gifts of God become a source of spiritual pride feeding our egos rather than a means of serving God's people. Spiritual gifts are given out by the Spirit for the mutual benefit of all, not for the selfish promotion of a few.

> Freedom is aristocratic and not democratic. Freedom of the minority generally involves repression of the majority by means of the law. This is the paradox of freedom in history.[11]   Nicolas Berdyaev

Legislation, control and manipulation became powerful tools in the hands of the clergy to control the public ministry and outreach of the Church. *The platform soon became a bully pulpit.* Fearing a loss of control of authority, religious leadership restricted more and more the movements and gifts of the Body along strict lines of control designed to achieve their own predetermined goals.

Religious leadership is too often guilty of preaching the principle of servant-leadership while slow to flesh out that truth in the midst of God's people. The robes of clericalism have the frightening tendency of giving those who wear them a false sense of spirituality and entitlement, and have ruined many a good child of God.

The Pillar of Conduct

Just as the Greeks and Romans negatively influenced the Church, so too did the Jews in the first century. The book of Acts chronicles the already emerging struggle between the long-awaited message of grace and the entrenched grasp of the law. The Jews, threatened by the message of Paul, consistently opposed him in every city. How could the freedom of grace be trusted to guide the human heart? Didn't history prove that the thoughts of man's heart were only evil continually? Using this logic, it was believed that new believers needed to remain within the fence of the law for their *own* safety.

Paul's impassioned exposition of the law in the book of Romans seems to have fallen on deaf ears. His passion for the church in Galatia had been forgotten. This great saint tutored by the Spirit of God in the wilderness—away from man's sway—recognized the devastation facing the new Church. Having begun in the spirit, the Body of Christ was being pulled toward the shifting sands of works of the flesh. Though, Paul fought this battle his whole life, man's love of law and order eventually triumphed. In the end, the Pharisees won the day. The Church that was birthed by amazing grace fell into the black hole of human effort. (This brings new meaning to the phrase "fall from grace.") And it has not yet fully moved to the other side, into the glorious light of grace in the face of Jesus. But I am seeing encouraging signs!

The Church's code of conduct has effectively repulsed the world and created no desire in them to be part of the clique. What the inner circle of the Church views as its witness to the world—purity—has only come off as narrow-minded bigotry. What we wear, where we go, what we watch, and what we read must all conform to the code, the established etiquette of the Church. This seemingly mindless conformity has no attraction to individuals looking for real relationship with a higher power. As Capon so succinctly puts it: The Church is full of forgiven sinners, but you have to draw the line somewhere to keep the riff raff out.

As a lesser light must give way to a greater light, so the light of the law must give way to the light of Messiah's grace. We must be willing to pull back the veil and allow the light of the most holy place to outshine the light of the candlestick in the outer room. The law must be swallowed up in the grace of God because it was fulfilled in Jesus. Key to spiritual growth is understanding that our good deeds can't get us into heaven, and bad deeds can't lock us out. As Thomas Merton said, you must "quit keeping the score altogether and surrender yourself with all your sinfulness to God who sees neither the score nor the scorekeeper but only his child redeemed by Christ."[12]

Traditions Extend the Franchise Through Time

The last pillar of the code that I want to look at is the traditions that have become an integral part of the environment of Christianity. It is so sad when the genuine spiritual experiences of one generation deteriorate, becoming the crusty customs of the next. Baptism, communion, foot washing, and worship—once powerful outward expressions of deep inner reality—lost much of their significance and potency, and became rote practices of a Church operating on auto pilot. The meetings of the Church, the government of the Church, the programs of the Church, and the celebrations of the Church are often more the matrix of a religious social club than the lifeblood of God's community.

If one is not careful, these once meaningful spiritual expressions can become encapsulated in time and extended as a franchise from one generation to the next. G.K. Chesterton said it well when he stated that traditions are "trusting to a consensus of common voices rather than to some isolated or arbitrary record. Tradition means giving votes to the most obscure of all classes, our ancestors. It is a democracy of the dead."[13]

Sunday after Sunday, believers gather together, sing the same songs, hear the same sermons, and walk out of the church meeting unchanged and unstirred. Echoes of the ancient language of Eden can be faintly heard, if one's ear is cocked just so. This constant exposure to religious rituals may, and often does, actually do more harm to the child of God than good. Occasionally in certain locales, one can sense the vitality of the primitive Church. But, by and large, we search in vain to find a house of God where God is truly present in a manifest way.

Where are the genuine gifts of the Spirit? Where are the true prophets and teachers of old? They have taken away our Lord and where have they laid Him? These are questions that are driving more and more *faithful* people to leave the Church. If the Church cannot break out of its love affair with the code, it may one day become irrelevant and obsolete. We must never forget that the Church does not exist to perpetuate itself, but to be a place where men and women can encounter God and freely share together the riches of that grace.

The rot of religion is based upon the continuous repetition of religious exercises that long ago have lost significance and meaning. The habitual replication of personal and corporate spiritual disciplines that were once rich with immediate impact eventually lose the vitality of their initial importance.[14]   Rufus M. Jones

A Fresh Stream of Spiritual Reality

A time is coming, perhaps it has even now begun, when man will grow weary of the religious code and will with a mighty shout break free from its hold. The redemptive periods in the history of the Church always came when a small remnant, daring to buck the tide, shattered the crust of customs, the chains of conformity, and the mindless submission to manmade authority. They were inevitably branded as rebels and written off by the Church as heretics. But as Jesus went outside the camp of religious thought—only to be put to death there by enraged guardians of the faith—these few brave souls have through the years been willing to follow Him there. And today there is a remnant who are willing to bear the reproach of Christ and to follow Him outside the camp. It is still only a stream, "more or less hidden and subterranean, of vital, inward, spiritual religion, dependent for its power of conviction and compassion, not on books, councils, hierarchies or doctrines, but on the soul's experiences of the eternal Realities."[15] They are being retaught by the Spirit the ancient language of Eden, and they will speak it far and wide.

The words of this chapter have been difficult to write. I know that not all churches are locked into the matrix of the code, but its reality encroaches upon all of us. Were it not for God's unrelenting love for His creatures and His determination that all things will be reconciled to Himself, we would have no cause for hope. He can hear the cry in the hearts of His people—a cry for the ancient ways.

We are "homesick" for our ancient home, where Father's face can be clearly seen, not dimly as through a glass. We long to feel the sweet winds of the Spirit blowing over our hungry, desperate souls. We cry out: "Abba, Father! Show us the way home!"

I believe He has heard our cry and will come suddenly. No man will be able to resist Him in that day. In the words of Mr. Belloc in

G.K. Chesterton's book, *Orthodoxy*: "Do not, I beseech you, be troubled about the increase of forces already in dissolution. You have mistaken the hour of the night: it is already morning."[16]

When the sleeping Bride awakens, she will be beautiful in her glory. The lovely ancient language of Eden will once again be spoken in clear, bell-like tones, filling the whole earth. And God will be glorified!

Endnotes

1. *God Is a New Language*, Sebastian Moore, The Newman Press, Westminster, Maryland, 1967, p. 9.

2. *Orthodoxy*, G.K. Chesterton, Harold Shaw Publishers, Colorado Springs, Colorado, 1994, p. 24.

3. *Abba's Child*, Brennan Manning, Navpress, Colorado Springs, Colorado, 1994, p. 77.

4. *Studies in Mystical Religion*, Rufus M. Jones, MacMillan and Co., London, 1903, p. 14.

5. *Christianity*, Hans Kung, Continuum, New York, 1995, p. 418.

6. *Christianity*, Hans Kung, p. 181.

7. *Language, Logic and God*, Frederick Ferre, Harper and Brothers, New York, 1961, p. 98.

8. *God is a New Language*, Sebastian Moore, The Newman Press, Westminster, Maryland, 1967, pp. 38-39.

9. *The Destiny of Man*, Nicolas Berdyaev, Harper Torchbooks, New York, 1960, p. 1.

10. *The Apostolic Fathers*, J.B. Lightfoot, Baker Books, Grand Rapids, Michigan, 1956, p. 84.

11. *The Destiny of Man*, Nicolas Berdyaev, p. 96.

12. *Abba's Child*, Brennan Manning, p. 27.

13. *Orthodoxy*, G.K. Chesterton, p. 47.

14. *Studies in Mystical Religion*, Rufus M. Jones, Macmillan & Co., London, 1923, p. 14.

15. *Studies in Mystical Religion*, Rufus M. Jones, p. 14.

16. *Orthodoxy*, G.K. Chesterton, p. 35.

It was the dismayed apostles, hollow men for whom God was dead, who proclaimed, in accents never heard before, the Living God. They proclaimed Him by being the indestructible community that sprang into being when the risen Lord appeared to his own.[1]

Sebastian Moore

I am about to reach my destination, but I am tired and my body is exhausted.
Help me to step toward the dawn to meet its splendor
My night is no more frightening, so is its darkness...
Pick up your remnants, brothers, the night is ending,
And come forth to welcome the light whose glory we missed so much...[2]

George Farah

The Christian Church is the entire community of the children of God. It is the actual Body of Christ, the Seed of Abraham, the House of the Living God, the Temple of the Holy Spirit. It has its life and power through the obedience of faith, it manifests to the world the Name of the Lord, the goodness and the glory of Him who called its members from darkness into His marvelous Light. Whenever such a Church is gathered, there is also Christ, its Head, who governs it, teaches, it, guards and defends it, works in it and pours His Life into its members. It expands and is enlarged by a process of organic growth under the organizing direction of the Holy Spirit.[3]

Caspar Schwenckfeld

CHAPTER 10

A NEW LANGUAGE FOR THE END TIMES

The day I was introduced to the outrageous, hilarious, and extravagant grace of Jesus was the beginning of an exciting, wonder-filled journey that will only end when I arrive home. As I ponder what lies in the days immediately ahead for me, I find myself thinking upon this verse: "And He appointed twelve, so that they would be with Him and that He could send them out to preach" (Mark 3:14). I have been so enjoying the secret place Father has me in; I'm swimming and splashing around in the pool of His amazing grace. The thought of having to move back out into church life has the power to really scare me. I guess, if I'm honest, I'd have to say I am afraid of being seduced back into the old ways of professional ministry. But I am feeling a gentle push on my back to get back out there and tell everyone I meet about this wonderful secret place of grace.

I find myself thinking on the law of the circular process. The spiritual reformers of the past declared that when a person has discovered the beginning of all things, he must return to his disordered world and proclaim the riches of the mysteries he has uncovered. Church history, as we've seen, is dotted with those who picked up the fallen baton of grace and sprinted for the finish line, passing it off to the next one God has waiting to carry it on.

Throughout the ages, there have been those courageous souls who succeeded in tearing off the tentacles of the code that bound them head to foot with its demands, rituals, and vanities. In the grip of grace, they wandered in the lonely, solitary places outside the walls of religion. They were listening for an echo, an answer to their cry! Under the grip of grace they wandered in the solitary places outside the walls of religion. They were searching for a place called Eden, where the will of man would be swallowed up into the will of Father, the place of perfect harmonies.

In agreement with the law of the circular process, these men and women lived in a dusky, somber, messy world where they exemplified the pure radiance of the heavenly realm they were contemplating. They became living vessels of the Spirit, testifying to a rich love they had discovered in the Father's face. You would think they would have been welcomed with open arms—but that was not the case. They were viewed as dissenters, troublemakers, questioning the authority of Church leaders.

As Capon declares, "The truth that makes us free is always ticking away like a time bomb in the basement of everybody's church."[4] Embedded in every church are men and women who have rediscovered the amazing power of grace, found in the person of Jesus, and they are looking for the appointed time to share this discovery. It remains to be seen whether the Church will receive the fresh word Father has given them, or if they will be driven "outside the camp."

Longing for the Ancient Ways

As in the days of those spiritual pioneers, we are living in a time when our own generation is growing soul sick of manmade traditions, hierarchical systems, lifeless liturgies, and spiritual superstars. You can discover them in out-of-the-way places, in backwoods towns, and in urban communities. They are tired of empty promises repetitively proclaimed from the platforms of men. Tired of pretending to see the emperor's new clothes when all that can be seen is the same old, same old.

There is a spiritual hunger in the people of God that is growing exponentially. Prayers are rising to the throne for a fresh infusion of life into the Church. Where is the vital life that propelled the early Church? Where are the true apostles and prophets who will build upon the Cornerstone and not upon their personal charisma? Where are those called by God to the ministry who will build *His* Kingdom and not *their* own kingdoms. We slap the title "apostolic ministry" on many an imitation.

We need true apostles who have experienced the wine of the Word, whose only desire is to know Christ and make Him known.

Jesus should be the *substance* of apostolic teaching and the *source* of apostolic work. What is more often found in apostolic ministry in our day is teaching on fivefold ministry or how to gain wealth or how to support your leaders. I have watched this phenomenon occur again and again—ministries have a way of taking on a life of their own. Men and women with a genuine calling to nurture the Body of Christ, finding themselves becoming better known and in increasing demand, start to realize they need more money to sustain their ministry and continue sharing their word. But as time goes by, that need for money begins to drive them instead of the needs of the Body.

What is Father doing while all this activity is going on in His name? What does He feel when He hears the voices of His children crying out for bread? What does He think when He comes to His House and He's not allowed to speak? What is He going to do about it?

One truth I have discovered throughout my Christian life is that God is a lot more relaxed about things than I am. I think I would tend to be like James and John, the sons of Zebedee, who walked with Jesus and were called the "Sons of Thunder"—"Call down fire, Lord!" But Jesus just told them to be cool. There is a time for everything under the sun, and only Father knows that time, and He is patient.

I, along with many others today, have my ears tuned, straining to catch a sound of that ancient language of Eden. And to my joy, I have detected voices here and there speaking with the recognizable accent of Eden. What are they saying? Grace! Unconditional love! Absolute acceptance! Scandalous love! Jesus!

Encounters With Heaven's Realm

If we can locate that ancient door and step through it, our beings will be filled with the wonder of Father's love. Abraham Heschel describes such a God encounter in these words:

> A tremor seizes our limbs; our nerves are struck, quiver like strings; our whole being bursts into shudders. But then a cry, wrested from our very core, fills the world around us, as if a mountain were suddenly about to place itself in front of us. It is one word: GOD. Not an emotion,

a stir within us, but a power, a marvel beyond us, tearing the world apart.[5]

We need an invasion of the loving-kindness of God to ravish us. I have been told most of my Christian life that we should not rely on emotions; in fact, we should not even trust them. Then what does that leave us? *Right where we are!* The frightening deadness that more and more people sitting in church are becoming aware of is the result of a faith lived in the realm of doctrine and religious activity. And if they don't soon find a life-giving antidote from their leaders, they are going to go searching in the highways and byways. Many already have walked out of the doors of the Church and are sitting in darkness, waiting for the light of His presence to break through and illumine the way once more. And you'd better know, their emotions will be very much in evidence.

Each experience with God is an internal whisper. As C.S. Lewis put it, "It is a whisper that will warehouse a shout."[6] The whisper-shouts of those who have experienced the Father's love will eventually drown out the cluttered speeches of religious men.

The Wine and the Word

Nor do people put new wine into old wineskins; otherwise the wineskins burst, and the wine pours out and the wineskins are ruined; but they put new wine into fresh wineskins, and both are preserved.   Matthew 9:17

When a person is drunk with wine, we say he is "under the influence." Well, the wine of God is a divine "influencer." It influences everything in a person's life. It acts as a spiritual stimulus, an inspiring intoxicant, an exhilarating elixir. When consumed in full strength, it has the capacity to create powerful change in the life of the imbiber. Onlookers describe those who have sat at Father's table and gotten drunk on the wine of His presence as scandalous, but they don't care, for they have lost their taste for the "mixed drinks" of men.

The primary ingredients in this spiritual elixir are the Spirit and the Word. Reading the Book of Acts, we see this dynamic duo in action. Their influence on the early Church is obvious, and the impact on the world is still clearly evident. Entfelder, one of the

great spiritual reformers of the 17th century, described these ingredients in this way:

> In every age, and in every land, the inner Word of God, the
> Voice of the Spirit speaking within, clarifying the mind
> and training the spiritual perceptions by a progressive ex-
> perience, has made for itself a chosen people and has gath-
> ered out of the world a little inner circle of those who know
> the Truth because it was formed within themselves.[7]

I just want to make sure we are on the same page here. I am
talking about the Word—Jesus. Not the Bible. John wanted to make
sure we knew that, so he started his Gospel account of Jesus with
that very explanation. The early Church went everywhere preaching
the Word. Paul put it more clearly when he said to the church at
Corinth that he only preached Christ. The early Church did not have
a New Testament to preach. They preached a person, and that person was the Word. When men and women received that Word it
began to work in their spirit man.

What is the nature of God's activity in the inward parts of
man? Who can explain how He moves upon the depths of our inner
man, changing and remolding us and creating a reflection of Himself? Who has stood on the sidelines and watched as He created new
life in the darkness of man's fallen soul? Man, with all his knowledge and ability, is powerless to change himself. Trying tirelessly to
pull himself up by his religious bootstraps only wears him out. True
spiritual change is a result of ongoing experiences with the Word of
God and the result of the Spirit's inward operation. It is an inward
work and it is the only key for individual and societal change.

> *Just as you do not know the path of the wind and how*
> *bones are formed in the womb of the pregnant woman, so*
> *you do not know the activity of God who makes all things.*
> Ecclesiastes 11:5

The Activity of God in the Church

The formation of the Church as a living organism is a result of
Father's work, not human initiative and effort. The creation of life in
the womb of a woman is a miracle of God's ingenuity. In the same
way, the creation of a church in the womb of the Spirit can happen
only by Father's will and purpose, and it is just as much a miracle.

Any church born out of the plans and purposes of a man is illegitimate, and even sometimes stillborn. It is not a legal son or heir. I am afraid we have many of these illegitimate and stillborn offspring in the world. But I also believe that God loves them too, just as Abraham loved Ishmael.

Only those born of the Spirit are responsive to the Word of God and have eyes to see the spiritual currents upon which the Spirit of God rides as He carries out the Father's purposes in the earth. We can look to Jesus to see the evidence of this statement. He saw those currents and declared that He only did what He saw the Father doing. Spiritual leaders would do well to dedicate their time and energy to using the eyes of their spirits to track and respond to the activity of God, rather than using all their energy to grow their churches or their traveling ministries.

The true Church of Christ is a masterpiece of the Spirit and a miracle of His grace, with the living Word being the life breath filling the Body. Leaders are simply meant to be midwives, assisting in the delivery and then watching over the growing Body. It is the Word and the Spirit that will bring back to us the ancient language of grace and institute a new spiritual order in the Body of Christ. As man exposes himself to the living Word—Jesus—and allows the Spirit to conform him to that Word, the desired growth will happen.

Then he answered and said to me,

> *"This is the **word** of the Lord to Zerubbabel saying, 'Not by might nor by power, but by My **Spirit**,' says the Lord of hosts."*   Zechariah 4:3-6, emphasis added

> *And when they had prayed, the place where they had gathered together was shaken, and they were all filled with the **Holy Spirit** and began to speak the **word of God** with boldness.*   Acts 4:31, emphasis added

> *And take the helmet of salvation, and the sword of the **Spirit**, which is the **word of God**.*
> Ephesians 6:17, emphasis added

The combination of the living Word and the Spirit is the only cure for what ails the Church in our days. We certainly do not need more rules or programs. We do not need better-trained leaders. We do not need more skilled musicians. We don't need bigger church buildings. What we do need—desperately need—is the dynamic presence of Jesus in our midst and a holy invasion of the Holy Spirit in everything that happens from the moment we enter the door of the church until we leave. Our cry must become: "Oh, come Word of God, enter the courts of Father's house, and once again turn over the tables of our religious activity."

Holy Spirit—Our Personal Tutor in the Ancient Language

"But when He, the Spirit of truth, comes, He will guide you into all the truth; for He will not speak on His own initiative, but whatever He hears, He will speak; and He will disclose to you what is to come."   John 16:13

The early Church depended on that Spirit for its very existence, not just for some revival meetings. Those believers knew they wouldn't have a clue what to do without the clear, moment-by-moment leading of the One sent to them by the departed Lord. They didn't just pray a prayer at the start of their meetings, asking for His blessing. They waited, usually in silence, for Him to come, sweep over them, and give them direction.

Perhaps many church meetings these days seem rote and stilted because we didn't get our directions from the Source. How many church committees and offices could be done away with if the Holy Spirit really were our guide and power? Without His continual presence, the Church has nothing to distinguish it from any other social club. We don't have the quality of music to be found in the concert halls of our cities. We don't have the warmth and camaraderie that can be found in most neighborhood bars. What do we have to offer the lost that they can't find anywhere else in the world?

As oxygen-rich air is the natural environment for all but sea creatures, so the spirit realm is the natural atmosphere for the Church. If she leaves that place and tries to breathe other air, she will die. This is exactly what happened to the primitive church in the second century. Having lost her way, she tried to live by another power. But life is not found in religion, only in the Word. When He is relegated to a token place in our lives or our churches, we begin gasping our last breath.

Jesus knew, I believe, that the cares and trouble they were going to face would cause His flock to forget His voice. He pictured them left alone at the mercies of the wolves baying at the door. So He and Father worked out a plan—Holy Spirit would come and abide with them. Jesus said that when He came, the Spirit of God would remind them daily of the things the Son said and did in those three short years. So on the Day of Pentecost when He came bursting into their midst, the flock knew that they were going to be all right as long as He stayed with them. They were careful in all they did to be sure it was by the leading and empowering of Holy Spirit. They did not want to offend Him. And He made sure they remembered the Son, and He built upon that foundation in their lives, expanding their understanding of the significance of the Son's words. They became a power to be reckoned with in their day because of the mighty working of the Spirit in their midst.

In too many churches we have no consciousness of the Spirit's presence. We talk about the gifts of the Spirit, the fruits of the Spirit, the anointing of the Spirit, the moving of the Spirit. But let's go back to the Source to see what the Holy Spirit is really here to do. In John 15:26, John records what Jesus told the disciples about this Comforter He was going to send. " 'When the Helper comes, whom I will send to you from the Father, that is the Spirit of truth who proceeds from the Father, He will testify about me.' " And in John 16:12 and 13, Christ tells the disciples: " 'I have many more things to say to you, but you cannot bear them now. But when He, the Spirit of truth, comes, He will guide you into all truth.' " And in John 16:14, Jesus continues, " 'He will glorify Me, for He will take of Mine and will disclose it to you.' "

Did Jesus mean the Spirit was going to come so they could teach about gifts, fruits, and tongues? It is very clear that the Holy Spirit was going to be given to us to keep us focused on Jesus, the Word. Jesus wasn't done with His teaching. Three years weren't near enough time to reveal all truth to us. There was more truth to be known, and the Spirit was going to take what was Jesus' and make it known to us. I want that truth. That is what my journey is about—to know all that Jesus wants me to know, about Him and about His plan for man.

It is not the church leaders' place to teach us all truth. Their calling is to be shepherds in the same manner as the Great Shepherd—leading in paths of safety, protecting from enemies, and making sure the sheep are healthy. But if the Spirit's dynamic moving in our midst is stifled, then the sheep have a decision to make—trust the powers of man or search out where the Holy Spirit is moving. The cessation of the gifts and the miraculous, which characterize the presence of Jesus, is not the result of the stopping of a dispensational time clock, but the product of having lost touch with the dimension of the other realm—the realm where God lives, the realm of the Spirit.

We must make room for the return of the empowering presence in the Church!

The Church—God's Love Letter to the World

You are our letter, written in our hearts, known and read by all men; being manifested that you are a letter of Christ, cared for by us, written not with ink but with the Spirit of the living God, not on tablets of stone but on tablets of human hearts.   2 Corinthians 3:2-3

God intended that each one of us become a unique and special word to those around us. We are all made in His image, but each one of us reflects that image in a unique way. Our life is a love letter to the world from the Father. Capon expressed it powerfully in these words: "The church was a womb, a matrix in which the Word of God himself gestated and from which he was delivered in written manifestations over a long period of time."[8]

The light of God's presence within His Body is refracted through the prisms of our own unique personalities and experiences. The spectrum of lights streaming from the prism of our lives is a unique manifestation and a testimony to the world of the reality of Christ. But the beauty of the lights of our lives cannot manifest the myriad colors of His Life if they are forced to pass through the opaqueness of a religious code.

The coming of the Spirit into our lives enables each one of us to express the ancient language of grace and mercy with our own special accents and idioms. The uniqueness of our personalities, the environment in which we live, and the experiences we have passed through have created our own unique message to the world. We don't have to duplicate someone else's message by trying to be like them. This only ruins the beauty of our own personal message. The church's insistence on conformity to its own rules and traditions obscures the beauty of each one's message to the world.

The church was meant to be a library filled with living literature that uniquely reveals the mysteries of Christ. These mysteries are revealed in a powerful way by the light of each believer's experience. Sadly, the library of the church has been filled with the cheap literature of legalism, division, judgmentalism, and empty clichés. We have created a powerful grid of religious piety and substructures of humanistic mindsets that obscures the richness of the spiritual word of Christ.

> We are in an age of faith, the Holy Spirit no longer writes
> gospels, except in our hearts; saintly souls are the pages,
> suffering and action the ink.[9]   Jean-Pierre De Caussade

As the church recovers more and more words of the ancient language of Eden, she will have a real message for the world—a message free from religious jargon. The message of Jesus and His fathomless love for all men will be heard in the rhythm of Eden's harmonic tones. I can hear the Spirit saying, "I'd like to teach the world to sing in perfect harmony."

> *"Can the Ethiopian change his skin or the leopard his
> spots?"*   Jeremiah 13:23

As I said earlier in the book, this question ate away at me for much of my life. In Bible college, our president's life message was dying to self, and I knew a student who upon hearing this message repeatedly went and camped out in a local cemetery with a sleeping bag and his Bible. He resolved he was not leaving there until he died. You guessed it—he was soon back in classes, very much alive. But he was just another case in point of a person struggling with the desire to change, to become someone better, only to collapse in hopelessness.

I think we can all say we have at one time or another tried the old tried and true (that's a cliché, by the way) methods for change: New Year's resolutions, self-denial, personal discipline, prayer and fasting, laying on of hands, and so on. Maybe they worked for you, but they didn't for me!

This is not some phenomenon. God's people have always known the constant battle of their outer man being, it seemed, directly opposed to what their born-again inner nature desired. Paul's words have echoed down through each generation.

> *For what I am doing, I do not understand; for I am not practicing what I would like to do, but I am doing the very thing I hate. ...Wretched man that I am! Who will set me free from the body of this death?*   Romans 7:15,24

Well, I'm happy to share with you the secret. *We can't change ourselves!* Isn't that good news? There is no method, no key, no prayer, no magic formula. There is only a person!

> *Thanks be to God through Jesus Christ our Lord!*
> Romans 7:25

It's been there right in front of our eyes every time we read through the book of Romans. The great apostle Paul, struggling with the very same "demons" we wrestle with—feelings of unworthiness, repeated sinning, guilt, and shame—finally received revelation. There is *no* condemnation to those found in Jesus. We simply cry, "*Abba!*" We are sons and daughters, joint heirs with Christ, and we do not have to fear our Father. He looks at our inner man and sees we want to be like His beloved Son, Jesus, and that's it for Him. We're home free! The law of the Spirit of life in Christ Jesus set us free from the condemnation of the law of sin and death.

Growth does not happen in our bodies by virtue of our efforts. Neither does it happen in our spirit men by effort or will. It takes place simply when something occurs in the depths of our beings. The Scriptures make it clear that God set times and seasons in the natural world, and the Bible makes it equally clear that He has times and seasons in the spirit world.

> *"As the branch ascends, the bud bursts, and the fruit ripens under the co-operation of influences from the outside air so man rises to the higher stature under invisible influences from without."*[10]   Henry Drummond

Growth does not happen as the result of spiritual knowledge or experiences, but it is a process that occurs over a lifetime. True, there are times when we have a significant spiritual encounter that jumpstarts change in our life, but for most people those experiences are rare. Change is a slow, steady process. This is the reason why the

Scriptures speak of endurance and patience. "And let endurance have its perfect result, so that you may be perfect and complete, lacking in nothing" (James 1:4).

Henry Drummond, perhaps best remembered as a gifted evangelist who assisted Dwight L. Moody during his revival campaigns, also was a lecturer in natural science. In his talks, he discussed the three laws of natural science. I believe these laws help us with the question, How does a man change his life? The three laws are: the law of *motion*, the law of *assimilation*, and the law of *influence.* Since I read these laws, I have been helped immensely in understanding the nature of spiritual growth. This knowledge greatly relieved still-hidden frustration in my growth process.

The Law of Motion

Every body continues in its state of rest, or of uniform motion in a straight line, except in so far as it may be compelled by impressed forces to change that state. This is also a first law of spiritual growth. *Every man's character remains as it is, or continues in the direction in which it is going, until it is compelled by impressed forces to change that state. Our failure has been the failure to put ourselves in the way of the impressed forces. There is a clay, and there is a Potter; we have tried to get the clay to mould the clay.*[11]   Henry Drummond

The clay is totally dependent on the hands of the Potter for the shaping of its existence. Only the Potter has the picture of the finished vessel in His mind. Unfortunately, what most of us have done is tried to get the clay to mold the clay—be it our own clay or someone else's clay. That's how we end up with mis-shapen pots. We must come to understand that changing a life is dependent on the forces in the spirit far beyond our puny efforts. What are these *impressed forces*?

Glory is an impressed force. "But we all, with unveiled face, beholding as in a mirror the glory of the Lord, are being transformed into the same image from glory to glory, just as from the Lord, the Spirit" (2 Cor. 3:18).

We live in a time when there is a lot of talk about the glory of God. What exactly is the glory of God? Remember Moses on Mount

Sinai having a personal tête-à-tête with God? Moses had the outrageous courage to ask God to show him His glory. Rather brash, don't you think? But God gave him his wish. He told Moses to squeeze himself into a big crack in a rock, and then God put His Hand in front of Moses to keep His glory from incinerating him on the spot. Then Moses heard these words as the Most High passed by: " 'The Lord, the Lord God, compassionate and gracious, slow to anger, and abounding in lovingkindness and truth; who keeps lovingkindness for thousands, who forgives iniquity, transgression and sin' " (Ex. 34:6-7).

The glory of God is found in the essence of who He is. God is love. God is grace. God is truth. Glory is not some ethereal, nebulous thing. It is very substantial and visible. It is substantial in the character of Christ's life, and it is visible in His acts toward man. The first Adam had the privilege of living in the glory of God, as he was always in His presence until he left the garden. The second Adam, too, lived in the Father's glory, but He shared it with Father. He laid it aside for a time while He lived among us, but it is once again His.

As we continuously read about and reflect on the grace and glory of God, we are promised that we will be transformed into that same image, from glory to glory. Drummond declared that "all men are mirrors." Our lives reflect the nature of the things we observe. As we experience God's grace in our lives and are changed from glory to glory, we are called to mirror that grace to others.

> *And the Word became flesh, and dwelt among us, and we saw His glory, glory as of the only begotten from the Father, full of grace and truth.*   John 1:14

> *For of His fullness we have all received, and grace upon grace.*   John 1:16

Suffering also is an impressed force. I realize this is a subject no one likes to talk about, and I confess it is not one of my favorite friends, but I have discovered that it doesn't have to be my enemy. This is probably one of the greatest struggles in the heart of man, be he believer or atheist. Again and again, you hear the charge leveled that if God really was love, there would be no seemingly random suffering in this world.

Like it or not, it is the calamities of life that push us, sometimes drag us, toward the place of change. We have all experienced the bewilderment that occurs when blessings seem suddenly to be suspended and we have no sense of His presence. We cry out for an explanation, and the heavens are as brass. We hear nothing. The trauma of losing someone we love, the drying up of finances, and the pain of sustained physical illness—we can all remember crying out to God for deliverance or at the very least, some kind of answer. Life is hard—we don't get that promotion we hoped for or we are laid off a job, our children drift away from us, cancer strikes us down. Yes, suffering is an impressed force.

Many of us were led to believe that Christians would not have to suffer like those in the world. It didn't take us long to find out the error of that belief. We have found out that we experience the same pain as those who don't know or don't love God. But even knowing that, we still suffer shock every time we are knocked up side the head with a new disaster. We still tend to react in anger toward the Lord because we know He could shield us from all these horrible things if He *wanted* to.

> *All discipline for the moment seems not to be joyful, but sorrowful; yet to those who have been trained by it, afterwards it yields the peaceful fruit of righteousness.*
>
> Hebrews 12:11

I read somewhere years ago, that we never learn anything new without pain. That truth comes to us in a negative form that we usually resist. After giving that some hard thought, I had to admit it had probably proved true in my life. Equally correct is that in passing through the valley of the shadow of death, the dark night of the soul, we discover a brokenness within us, a good brokenness, and a new sense of closeness to the Lord. In the shattering of our peace and our dreams, we often discover new truths never before known. We find that the night became a pathway, a birth canal if you will, into a place we have never before been. We never could have reached that place unless we walked through the dark regions.

I remember so well the words of an old Barry McGuire tune that I heard shortly after my release from prison:

> I walked a mile with pleasure,
> She chattered all the way,

And left me none the wiser
For all she had to say.

I walked a mile with sorrow,
Never a word said she,
But oh the things I learned
When sorrow walked with me.[12]

My first days in that communist prison years ago are still so clear in my mind. Besides the shock of our world being turned terrifyingly upside down, Micki and I were reeling with the sense of abandonment by Father. We knew something about suffering; we weren't total novices to the concept, but this was beyond the normal pain. We had only been in that country a couple of years, and God had worked all sorts of miracles, confirming His pleasure with us. Now it was all stripped away. But acceptance, or perhaps it was resignation, finally brought a sort of peace—the kind of peace that comes from knowing there is nothing you can do. Either God does something, or there you will stay.

One day, I was lying on my cot reading the Psalms in my little Bible that I managed to keep hidden in my cell. David was ranting and raving just like me, complaining about his enemies and God's absence. As I reached the end of that passage, David in one of his about-faces said, "But I have trusted in Your lovingkindness; my heart shall rejoice in Your salvation" (Ps. 13:5). Something leaped inside me at that moment, and I sensed a voice saying my night was about to end. Only a week later, by a series of sovereign moves of God's Hand, I was expelled from Mozambique and on my way home.

I wouldn't want you to think, "Oh, he got the lesson and then lived happily ever after!" As I told you earlier, I went back to life as usual ("Thank God that's over!") and never really processed my experience in Africa.

It was only much later in my life, after a couple of more devastating blows, that the light dawned. My spirit had been enlarged—it was deeper and wider, and fuller than it had ever been—and I hadn't even seen it happening. Most of us have very puny souls, like muscles that seldom get exercised. The materialism and self-centeredness of this age have caused them to wither up. But when our lives collide with the impressed force of suffering, those muscles begin to enlargement. Again, the Psalmist of Israel, who had suffered so much put it this way: "Answer me when I call, O God of my righteousness! Thou hast relieved me in my distress; be gracious to me and hear my prayer" (Ps. 4:1). The Hebrew word for distress means "trouble" or "pressure," and the word for relieved is "enlarge" or "make room for." So David was saying what we were just saying—in pressure you have enlarged me. Trouble can become a friend in God's Hand.

Augustine picked up on this same theme in his writings. His mother dramatically influenced his life in a positive way. She was the support and encouragement that helped him fulfill his destiny. At her death, he was thrown into a deep depression. Though devastating, that experience helped him come to the revelation that life's disappointments do have a mysterious way of enlarging a man's soul, making him stronger and more confident in his faith. In *Confessions*, Augustine wrote these words: "The house of my soul is narrow—O enlarge it, that Thou mayest enter in!"

We are not called upon to *enjoy* pain, but to *endure* it, understanding that in the pressures of life we are being transformed into the image of our beloved Jesus, who also suffered. Peter said it this way, "To the degree that you share the sufferings of Christ, so that also *at the revelation of His glory* you may rejoice with exultation" (1 Peter 4:13).

The Law of Assimilation

The things that we put into our spirit will be reflected in our life. This Law of Assimilation is the second, and by far the most impressive truth, which underlies the formula of sanctification. The truth that men are not only mirrors, but that these mirrors so far from being mere reflectors of the fleeting things they see, transfer into their own inmost substance, and hold in permanent preservation the things that they reflect.[13]   Henry Drummond

We hold in permanent preservation the things that we reflect— this is the power of the law of assimilation. By what power do we retain those things upon which we reflect? In computer lingo we say, *garbage in, garbage out.* Input into a computer is retained in its memory banks for immediate access. Man is a living computer.

There is a wealth of memories stored within us—truths we have learned, experience we have had, people we have met, words we have heard, places we have visited, sounds, smells, and so on. And just like a computer, our memory banks are not selective, in that they hold the good, the bad, and the ugly. These memories are not simply stored in our minds, they have gone into our very psyches and shaped us—the way we think, the way we feel, and the way we act.

There are many forces in each of our lives that we have no control over. Stuff happens. But we are responsible for a lot of the other forces that impress us. There is a saying, "You are what you eat." While that is true, it is also true to say: "You are what you read. You are what you listen to. You become like those you hang out with."

I don't want you to think I am talking about the old tenets of the code that seek to legalistically regulate us. I am just saying that sometimes hanging with "bad" people can exert a powerful impression on our souls. And sometimes associating with the so-called "good" people can have an equally negative influence on us. Look at the people Jesus hung out with. He seemed to prefer the company of the rejects of society to that of the religiously "good" of His day. So labels don't mean anything. Being sensitive to the cursor of the Spirit pulsating on the screen of our hearts should be our guide as to what we're inputting into our souls.

We want to be directly under the loving influence of Jesus—hearing His voice, reading His words, contemplating His life. As we do this, He will explain the Father to us. We will be drawn into that intimate circle that Jesus promised was our rightful place—right there with Him and Father—and be changed into His image without even trying. Paul's driving passion was to draw others into this love fest he had discovered. As His own character was being transformed into the nature of God, an urge was burning within him to nurture that life in others. "My children, with whom I am again in labor until Christ is formed in you" (Gal. 4:19).

The Law of Influence

It is by the Law of Influence that we become like those whom we habitually admire: these had become like because they habitually admired. Through all the range of literature, of history, and biography this law presides. Men are all mosaics of other men.[14]   Henry Drummond

No man is an island. No one exists in this life in a vacuum. Therefore we are all results of the influence or impact other people have had on our lives, for good or for evil. Those who have been abused, ridiculed, scorned, or rejected bear deep wounds in their souls. And the real tragedy is, they have *become* those wounds. They are damaged people who will, without a divine intervention, damage others. Then on the other hand, there are those who have only known acceptance and love and have become sources of love and light to others. Drummond spoke of the powerful impact Jesus had on His ragamuffin disciples.

> A few raw, unspiritual, uninspiring men were admitted to the inner circle of His friendship. The change began at once. Day by day we can almost see the first disciples grow. First there steals over them the faintest possible adumbration of His character, and occasionally, very occasionally, they do a thing, or say a thing that they could not have done or said had they not been living there. Slowly the spell of His Life deepens. Reach after reach of their nature is overtaken, thawed, subjugated, sanctified.

> Their manners soften, their words become more gentle, their conduct more unselfish. As swallows who have found a summer, as frozen buds the spring, their starved humanity bursts into a fuller life. They do not know how it is, but they are different men.

> One day they find themselves like their Master, going about and doing good. To themselves it is unaccountable, but they cannot do otherwise. They were not told to do it, it came to them to do it. But the people who watch them know well how to account for it. "They have been," they whisper, "with Jesus." Already even, the mark and seal of His character is upon them. "They have been with Jesus." Unparalleled phenomenon, that these poor fishermen should remind other men of Christ! Stupendous victory

and mystery of regeneration that mortal men should suggest to the world, God!"[15]

The friends I have been blessed to have in my life have had a deep impact upon me. Even when I withdrew into my hole, licking my wounds, they were always there for me, making their love known. They have fleshed out Jesus time and again. Unconditional acceptance and love is an increasingly rare thing in this world, so it is to be highly valued when offered.

The other major influence in my life has been books. I view them as signposts along the way that other pioneers have left to help others in their journeys. In the last three to four years, Micki and I found little in church to help us in our quest for reality, so we began to read. We read, and we read, and we read. We read Henry Drummond, C.S. Lewis, Brennan Manning, Robert Farrar Capon, St. John of the Cross, S.D. Gordon, Geoffrey Bull, Henri Nouwen, Philip Yancey, Flannery O'Connor, Father Joseph Girzone, Scholem Asch, Paul Tillich, Rufus M. Jones, John Shea, *and* my precious Bible.

These dear brothers and sisters have left their mark on us. But the deepest fingerprint they have impressed upon us is Jesus—in a way we're never seen or been taught about Him. They have, through the inspiration of the Holy Spirit, introduced us to a Lord we never knew—and *He is beautiful!*

A New (or Old) Breed of Christians

This is a great day to be alive! God's grace came crashing into my life, tearing down manmade barriers in my spirit, and I now watch, with growing excitement as I see Him doing the same everywhere I go. The ancient gate to the garden is swinging wide, and God's people are finding their way to the tree of life. That tree, you see, is the key to the whole story. You first see it in the second chapter of the Bible, and then you next see it in the last chapter of Revelation, just a short distance away from the throne of God. The end is truly found in the beginning.

If the Church is to survive, to be that Bride Jesus is longing for, she is going to have to free God's people, as they renounce the code and follow the Lamb wherever He goes. A new breed of Christians—men and women who have touched eternity and are experiencing the rediscovered truth of God's scandalous love—will touch this world with the lost message of grace. The language of sin, shame, and guilt that the Church has communicated to a world that already stands condemned will be, I believe, replaced with the ancient language of Eden.

> There is a lot of teaching in the earth today about the Body of Christ...how God has sent forth His gifts upon His people, to bind them together in a common fellowship, and to endue them with power and anointing, that they might become vital members of the glorious Body of Christ. And yet, sad to say, there seems to be very little evidence in our assemblies of the mighty, abiding Presence of Christ, and of His Lordship in the lives of His people. I think that the reason is quite evident. We want His blessings and His gifts and His miracle working power, and we cry out for more and more of these...but He answers back: "My desire is that you should come into total union with Myself, and walk in My truth, in My life, in My holiness, in My patience, in My longsuffering, in My kindness, in My mercy, in My love. I want you to be ONE WITH ME in all things.[16]   George Warnock

As God is gathering a remnant, one by one, out of a dead religious system—they will gather together around Jesus, and the language they will be heard speaking will be the ancient language of Eden—the language of love, grace, and mercy.

Endnotes

1. *God Is a New Language*, Sebastian Moore, The Newman Press, Westminster, Maryland, 1967 p. 48.

2. www.webhome.idirect.com/~ffarah/echo.html.

3. *Spiritual Reformers of the 16th and 17th Century*, Rufus M. Jones, The MacMillan Company, 1914, p. 78.

4. *The Mystery of Christ*, Robert Farrar Capon, Eerdmans, Grand Rapids, Michigan, 1993, p. 140.

5. *Dangerous Wonder*, Michael Yaconelli, Navpress, Colorado Springs, Colorado, 1998, p. 107.

6. *The Quotable Lewis*, Wayne Martindale, Jerry Root, Tyndale House Publishers, Wheaton, Illinois, 1989, p. 424.

7. *Spiritual Reformers of the 16th and 17th Century*, Rufus M. Jones, The MacMillan Company, 1914, p. 41.

8. *The Fingerprints of God*, Robert Farrar Capon, Eerdmans, Grand Rapids, Michigan, 2000, p. 8.

9. *The Sacrament of the Present Moment*, Jean-Pierre De Caussade, p. 101.

10. *The Changed Life*, Henry Drummond, www.ccel.org/ccel/drummond/greatest.IV.html.

11. *The Changed Life*, Henry Drummond, www.ccel.org/ccel/drummond/greatest.IV.html.

12. Source unknown.

13. *The Changed Life*, Henry Drummond, www.ccel.org/ccel/drummond/greatest.IV.html.

14. *The Changed Life*, Henry Drummond, www.ccel.org/ccel/drummond/greatest.IV.html.

15. *The Changed Life*, Henry Drummond, www.ccel.org/ccel/drummond/greatest.IV.html.

16. *The Refiner's Fire, The Call to Intimate Relationship*, George Warnock, Rare Christian Books, Dixon, Missouri, no copyright, p. 54.

To contact the author you may write him at:

Donald L. Milam
2958 Fillmore Drive
Chambersburg, PA 17201

Or you may e-mail him at:

dlm@destinyimage.com

Or visit his Web site at:

www.radicalgrace.org

Also by
DON MILAM

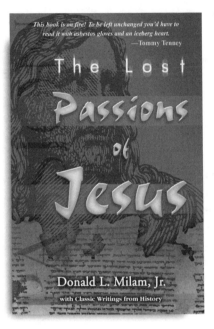

This book is on fire! To be left unchanged you'd have to read it with asbestos gloves and an iceberg heart.
—Tommy Tenney

The Lost
Passions
of
Jesus

Donald L. Milam, Jr.
with Classic Writings from History

THE LOST PASSIONS OF JESUS

What motivated Jesus to pursue the cross? What inner strength kept His feet on the path laid before Him? Time and tradition have muted the Church's knowledge of the passions that burned in Jesus' heart, but if we want to—if we dare to—we can still seek those same passions. Learn from a close look at Jesus' own life and words and from the writings of other dedicated followers the passions that enflamed the Son of God and changed the world forever!

ISBN: 0-9677402-0-7